GINGER

Move YOURSELF, Move the WORLD

7 Practical Steps to Become A Spectacular Person

The opinions expressed in this manuscript are solely the opinions of the author and do not represent the opinions or thoughts of the publisher. The author has represented and warranted full ownership and/or legal right to publish all the materials in this book.

Move Yourself, Move the World
7 Practical Steps to Become A Spectacular Person
All Rights Reserved.
Copyright © 2014 Ginger Richards
v2.0

Cover Photo © 2014 thinkstockphotos.com. All rights reserved - used with permission.

This book may not be reproduced, transmitted, or stored in whole or in part by any means, including graphic, electronic, or mechanical without the express written consent of the publisher except in the case of brief quotations embodied in critical articles and reviews.

Outskirts Press, Inc.
http://www.outskirtspress.com

ISBN: 978-1-4787-3435-2

Outskirts Press and the "OP" logo are trademarks belonging to Outskirts Press, Inc.

PRINTED IN THE UNITED STATES OF AMERICA

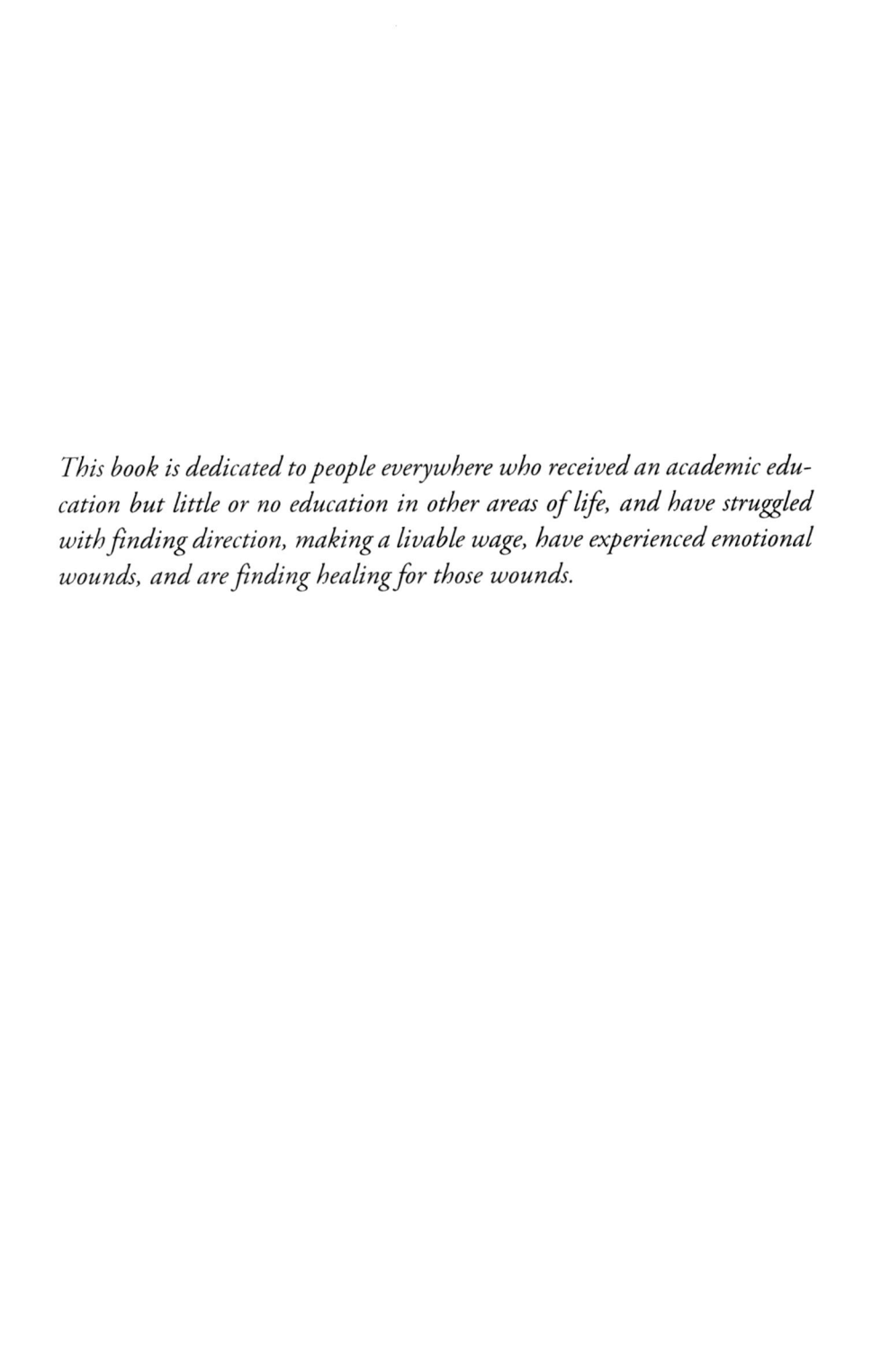

This book is dedicated to people everywhere who received an academic education but little or no education in other areas of life, and have struggled with finding direction, making a livable wage, have experienced emotional wounds, and are finding healing for those wounds.

Contents

Acknowledgments i
    Introduction iii
    How to Use This Book iii
    Motivation and Self-Discipline iv

1: Admire 1
2: Aspire 10
3: Acquire 21
4: Inquire 33
5: Require 44
6: Perspire 56
7: Inspire 66

Appendices

Appendix A—Goals and Desires 75
Appendix B—Expectations 81
Appendix C—Disappointment 85

Appendix D—Taking Up Defenses 89

Appendix E—Taking Up Offenses 91

Appendix F—Strategies for HALT 93

Appendix G—Thinking/Reacting 95

Appendix H—Requiring More of Yourself 97

Appendix I—Winning and Losing 105

Appendix J—Respect 107

Acknowledgments

I would like to thank Dr. Jay Fernlund for his hours of reading, proofing, and critiquing the manuscript. His help with explaining inductive and deductive reasoning is priceless. I would also like to thank him for the encouragement he has given me through the years, not only in writing this book, but in my life in general. He has truly been a Barnabas in my life, and I am extremely grateful for his years of service at the church we attend. May the Lord continue to bless him and all that he does.

The translations of the Bible I used are The New American Standard and The New Living Translation.

Introduction

In the pages that follow you will find several elements. Each chapter has a one-word title. First, you will see what part of speech that word is. Next, are definitions for that word. Third, you will read a challenge, and then you will read a little about me. This is not an autobiography. I simply use my past as the example. My intention is that you see both my errors and my triumphs, and that you will learn from what I offer. My life has been my own journey, and I have learned some important things along the way. I write them here so that your life journey can be altered for the better.

Finally, there are Bible verses and quotes for you to ponder and glean from their wisdom.

As you read, it may seem to you that things are being repeated in several chapters, especially in the chapters on acquiring, requiring, and perspiring. This is because all of these words are intertwined—each one is important to the others. I've tried to give each chapter a different emphasis, yet maintain a cohesive structure.

In an effort to make the chapters a reasonable length, I have added appendices which contain much more information that just could not be fit into the chapters.

How to Use This Book

Though this book is short enough to read in one sitting, I suggest that the reader read only one chapter a day. This will allow you time to think about what you've read and to begin working on the challenge for that day. You could also view the chapter titles as a word for the day, each day for a week. If there are too many quotes, read a few, and then read the remaining quotes at a later time.

Motivation and Self-Discipline

With any course of study, motivation and self-discipline are essential. You must be motivated to begin something, and desire to complete it, and disciplined enough to follow through to the end. Many people like to start things, but never see them through to completion. There are many reasons for this. But I think lack of self-discipline is one BIG factor. It takes about a month of doing something repeatedly before it becomes a habit. A habit is something you do without effort, and without even thinking about it. Brushing your teeth after meals is something you first have to motivate yourself to do. Then, you have to discipline yourself to continue to do it, even when you don't feel like it. After a month of repeating this practice every day, several times a day, it develops into a habit. After it has become a habit, you don't have to think about doing it—you just do it.

Because we don't discipline ourselves to complete something, we start excusing ourselves from doing it at all. Excuses abound. "It's too hard." "I don't know how to do it." "I need help," which usually means "Will you do it for me?" "I don't have the time." "I have too many things to do." "I lost interest." "I'm too tired." "I don't want to do that." "I don't feel like doing it."

These excuses apply to everything under the sun—homework, exercising, practicing an instrument, writing a book, reading a book, doing housework or chores, taking care of a pet, etc.

Really, the only way that anything gets done is that there is an internal motivation to begin and the self-discipline to finish. So it will be in reading this book and putting into practice these action words. You will need to motivate yourself to start reading and to continue till the end. You will also need to discipline yourself to act on the challenge that is presented. Before you begin this journey, read these quotes on motivation and self-discipline and let the words of wisdom from others plant the seeds of growth and maturing in your mind.

"Better to light one small candle than to curse the darkness."

~ Chinese Proverb

"You must motivate yourself EVERY DAY."

~ Matthew Stasior

"The best motivation always comes from within."

~ Michael Johnson

"There is no luck except where there is discipline."

~ Irish Proverb

"If you would live your life with ease; do what you ought, not as you please."

~ Anonymous

"He who conquers himself has won a greater victory than he who conquers a city."

~ Proverbs

"Let him who would move the world first move himself."

~ Socrates

1

Admire

Admire - verb
Definition:
1. To regard with wonder and delighted approval
2. To have a high opinion of; esteem

The Challenge
Search for a good role model—a person who has any of the following: positive character qualities, has influenced history in positive ways, was or is a good citizen, was or is self-controlled, was or is a leader, or has accomplished something you can look up to.

When I was young, I was too caught up in my own world to even think about admiring anyone. Life, for me, was about surviving in my family, and being happy, or thriving with my friends. My family was what we now call dysfunctional. Growing up in my family was difficult—that's why I say I was focused on surviving. Friends were much more nurturing than my own parents were. I was pretty happy with my friends, and that's why I use the word *thriving*. I didn't think in those terms then—surviving and thriving—but, looking back, I can now say that that pretty much sums up my childhood.

A second reason for not developing an admiration for anyone was that every adult I knew seemed strict, orderly, and emotionless. There was not much about those qualities that I wanted to admire. Everyone from teachers, and church people, to the local crossing guard, all seemed to be the same kind of people. They seemed like the same person, cookie-cutter people, just in different bodies. There were no apparent differences in their characters, attitudes, or behavior that stood out—the kind of thing that makes you notice and say, "I want to be like him/her." Sure, there were some adults that did some nice things, like give you Christmas presents, or give you a ride to church if needed, but, all in all, they didn't go out of their way to see to a child's needs or problems, or to be a soft, safe place for a child. That was the parents' responsibility and domain, and if parents were not doing an adequate job, then, the needs and problems did not get addressed. And there was no soft, safe place.

I will say that most of the adults seemed to be responsible—meaning that they held jobs and seemed to have good families. They had positions or good standing in the church or community . . . Although appearances are deceiving, and you never know what goes on in people's homes when they're behind closed doors. But, as a child, you normally believe what you are told and what you see. Even if what was seen *was* the real deal, it was not enough for me to admire any of them or want to be like them. That was poor reasoning on my part. I could have looked beyond my own world of adults.

A third reason for not developing an admiration for anyone is that, while I was an excellent reader, I didn't like to read on my own. I only became interested in biographies in junior high and high school. When I read about anyone, it was just to learn about them and not because I wanted to discover good qualities about them.

Today, however, the opportunities to see and experience people with diverse character qualities are abundant. We have grown and learned to not only accept differences, but to enjoy and celebrate them. If you look around, you should be able to find people who work hard, people who finish what they start, people who love life and enjoy living, people who care about people, people who give time, people who give money, people who stand up for their convictions, people who are authentic, and the list goes on. So, my challenge to you is to think of someone around you—maybe you know them personally, maybe you don't—that has some quality that you would like to develop in your life. Identify the quality, for example, honesty. Next, learn all you can about honesty—old sayings like "honesty is the best policy"—and then think about what that really means. Then, dig deeper. Search for people in history that exemplified that quality. For example, for honesty, we know that Abraham Lincoln was known as "Honest Abe." Then, read biographies on that person and gain an understanding of his/her life and how they developed that quality or characteristic.

When you visit a library, ask the librarian to recommend biographies of the people who have that specific quality.

When you are given an assignment at school to read about a specific person, read with the intent to find a positive character quality as well as the basic information that is given. This will deepen your understanding of this person. For instance, Thomas Edison failed over 1,000 times before perfecting the incandescent lightbulb. He showed perseverance and determination.

As you work on developing this one character quality, go back to the list and choose another one. Read about that quality and find people who had it. Again, read biographies of those who were well-known for that quality. Develop this one into your life. Then, keep adding more positive character qualities into your life.

Just one caution, though. Try to avoid focusing on the current pop culture stars and icons. Admiring someone's fame, wealth, or "bling" and wanting to be like them is not what I'm talking about. Many of the rich and famous have trouble staying out of jail, staying sober, and staying married. Many use their fame and wealth to their own detriment. If you do choose to read about them, look at their shortcomings and determine that these are **not** the character qualities that you want in your life. If the book talks about their struggles and hardships, then pay attention to how they handled them. Good results don't necessarily mean that they employed good practices to gain the results. The end does not justify the means.

MOVE YOURSELF, MOVE THE WORLD

Even when reading about biblical characters, remember they too had faults and problem areas. The Bible doesn't sugarcoat anyone, and the bad as well as the good is recorded. The bad is there to show us what we should avoid. The good is there to show us their faith and obedience to God.

"Follow the steps of good men instead, and stay on the paths of the righteous."

~ Proverbs 2:20

"If thou art a man, admire those who attempt great things, even though they fail."

~ Lucius Annaeus Seneca

"Good character is more to be praised than outstanding talent. Most talents are, to some extent, a gift. Good character, by contrast, is not given to us. We have to build it, piece by piece—by thought, choice, courage, and determination."

~ H. Jackson Brown

"Everyone tries to define this thing called Character. It's not hard. Character is doing what's right when nobody's looking."

~ J. C. Watts

"When the character of a man is not clear to you, look at his friends."

~ Japanese Proverb

"When you choose your friends, don't be short-changed by choosing personality over character."

~ W. Somerset Maugham

ADMIRE

"Associate yourself with people of good quality, for it is better to be alone than in bad company."

~ Booker T. Washington

"You can easily judge the character of a man by how he treats those who can do nothing for him."

~ James D. Miles

"There are times when a man should be content with what he has but never with what he is."

~ William George Jordan

"Hard work spotlights the character of people: some turn up their sleeves, some turn up their noses, and some don't turn up at all."

~ Sam Ewig

"Character is like a tree and reputation like a shadow. The shadow is what we think of it; the tree is the real thing."

~ Abraham Lincoln

"Reputation is what the world thinks a man is; character is what he really is."

~ Anonymous

"The most important of life's battles is the one we fight daily in the silent chambers of the soul."

~ David O. McKay

"One cannot think crooked and walk straight."

~ Anonymous

MOVE YOURSELF, MOVE THE WORLD

"Are you fit company for the person you wish to become?"

~ Anonymous

"Wealth stays with us a little moment if at all: only our characters are steadfast, not our gold."

~ Euripides

"Sow a thought, and you reap an act;
Sow an act, and you reap a habit;
Sow a habit, and you reap a character;
Sow a character, and you reap a destiny."

~ Charles Reade

"Character cannot be developed in ease and quiet. Only through experience of trial and suffering can the soul be strengthened, ambition inspired, and success achieved."

~ Helen Keller

"A man's character may be learned from the adjectives which he habitually uses in conversation."

~ Mark Twain

"In words are seen the state of mind and character and disposition of the speaker."

~ Plutarch

"Nearly all men can stand adversity, but if you want to test a man's character, give him power."

~ Abraham Lincoln

ADMIRE

"Character, not circumstances, makes the man."

~ Booker T. Washington

"Laws control the lesser man . . . Right conduct controls the greater one."

~ Mark Twain

"Many a man's reputation would not know his character if they met on the street."

~ Elbert Hubbard

"Character is what you have left when you've lost everything you can lose."

~ Evan Esar

"Character must be kept bright as well as clean."

~ Lord Chesterfield

"He who walks with wise men will be wise, but the companion of fools will suffer harm."

~ Proverbs 13:20

"Wisdom is knowing what to do next, skill is knowing how to do it, and virtue is doing it."

~ David Starr Jordan

"Who you are speaks so loudly I can't hear what you're saying."

~ Ralph Waldo Emerson

MOVE YOURSELF, MOVE THE WORLD

"You can tell more about a person by what he says about others than you can by what others say about him."

~ Leo Aikman

"You can tell the character of every man when you see how he receives praise."

~ Lucius Annaeus Seneca

"Put more trust in nobility of character than in an oath."

~ Solon

"A man's own manner and character is what most becomes him."

~ Marcus Tullius Cicero

"Good habits formed at youth make all the difference."

~ Aristotle

Below, and on the next page, is a list of positive character qualities to help you in your quest.

If you are unsure of the meaning of a word, look it up in the dictionary. Finding out the meaning may help you to determine if this is a character quality that you would like to have.

List of Positive Qualities

Accuracy	Expressiveness	Persistence
Adaptability	Fairness	Perseverance
Amiability	Flexibility	Persuasiveness
Attentiveness	Forgiveness	Punctuality
Availability	Frankness	Purposefulness
Compassion	Frugality	Resoluteness
Confidence	Generosity	Resourcefulness
Contentment	Gentleness	Respectfulness

ADMIRE

Cooperativeness
Courage
Courtesy
Creativity
Decisiveness
Dependability
Determination
Diligence
Discipline
Discretion
Efficiency
Endurance
Enthusiasm

Gratefulness
Honesty
Hospitality
Humility
Initiative
Joyfulness
Kindness
Loyalty
Meekness
Neatness
Obedience
Objectivity
Patience

Responsiveness
Responsibility
Self-control
Sensitivity
Sincerity
Thoroughness
Tolerance
Truthfulness
Wisdom

Interesting People to Read About

<u>Historical/Biblical</u>
Abraham   Ruth
Joseph   Esther
Moses   Daniel
Joshua   John
David   Paul

<u>Inventors/Scientists</u>
George Washington Carver
Madame C. J. Walker
Nikola Tesla
Thomas Edison
Albert Einstein

<u>Historical/Nonbiblical</u>
Martin Luther
Elizabeth I
Shakespeare
George Washington
William Wilberforce
Benjamin Franklin
Abraham Lincoln
Frederick Douglass
Harriet Tubman
Martin Luther King Jr.

<u>Artistic/Musical</u>
Leonardo da Vinci
Michelangelo
J. S. Bach
W. A. Mozart
L. van Beethoven
A. Dvorak
Mather Brown
Le Chevalier de Saint-Georges
Scott Joplin
Samuel Coleridge-Taylor

2

Aspire

Aspire ~ verb
Definition:
To have ambition

The Challenge
Have the drive and determination (the ambition) to find out who you are, what you're good at, what your strengths are, and what you want to accomplish—and then, be the best that you can be. Be the "you" that God designed you to be.

As a child I had a lot of career dreams, but I didn't really aspire to anything. For a while I envisioned myself being a concert pianist. I also wanted to take dance lessons and maybe become a dancer. At one time, I briefly wanted to be a jockey. All through grade school I had a talent for art. In fourth grade, I became interested in traveling and wanted to be an artist to pay for my world travels.

Sometimes, when I thought I might like to try a new thing—like running—a teacher, or someone else, would usually shoot down the idea. I knew I was chubby and not terribly athletic, but I would have loved to have participated in some races. The teacher thought I would be embarrassed if I didn't do well because of my weight, not realizing that it was her remark in front of the whole class that was embarrassing.

ASPIRE

By junior high, I had no dreams left in me. All the ones I had had previously were shot down. So during most of my school years, I stayed in the background. I didn't try terribly hard to be good at anything. However, in eighth grade, my English teacher did recognize me as being a very fast reader and recommended that I take X English in high school.

In high school, I did begin to develop one aspiration or desire—to be a Madrigal. I loved to sing and was in the progression of choirs from freshman year to senior year. It was in my senior year that I became a Madrigal. In my high school, Madrigals was a sixteen member ensemble. It was eight part harmony with two people on each part. Sometimes we did a cappella (no accompaniment) music and sometimes we had piano accompaniment. I loved it. I learned so much about vocal music in that year alone. But, being a Madrigal couldn't fuel any flames of future aspirations for my life after high school. You see, I found out that to pursue vocal music in college, you needed to play the piano. That made no sense to me. I had a hard time mastering the piano, and I couldn't see why I should be denied a chance to pursue one without the other. I lost the will to continue my vocal music education. So, I graduated from high school with no dreams or aspirations and no direction for my life. I took the first job I could get and struggled with minimum wage paying jobs most of my adult life. I went from job to job, never really liking them enough to stay for very long. I also really never knew the kind of job or career that would be a good fit for me.

At age nineteen, I took a ten-day vacation to Puerto Rico with my sister. That was the beginning of a short span of world travels. When I was twenty-one, I took a three-week trip to Israel. It was a shortened college class—a full semester crammed into three weeks. On the return trip, we spent a weekend in London, England. The following year, I went on a three-week tour of Europe. The tour group visited France, Switzerland, Italy, Austria, Germany, Luxembourg, Belgium, and Holland. All three of my trips were wonderful experiences that I would highly recommend to anyone. My brief travels were exciting, educational, and, at times, entertaining.

During my early twenties, I aspired to be or do very little. I worked and travelled. I hadn't learned much about myself or any talents God had given me, other than singing. I had no dreams. At age twenty-four, I had my first child, and traveling was then put on hold.

It wasn't till I was in my thirties that I began looking at who I was, what I loved, and what I was good at.

There are many things you need to know about yourself. Some of this knowledge is helpful while you are in school, such as your learning modality and multiple intelligences. Other knowledge is helpful in developing good relationships, such as knowing your emotional needs, your particular love languages, and your specific apology language. Still, other information is useful to know because it identifies your strengths and helps direct you to the right job or career.

It is also important to uncover your passions in life, your purpose for being here, and to identify, and then pursue, your dreams. I would also recommend that God be included in your search for your identity, passions, purpose, and dreams. For it is He who created you, gave you life, put you together as a unique individual, and placed dreams within your soul. He alone has the blueprint of your life. So make sure you consult the master architect along the way.

Once you are convinced of God's purpose and plan for your life, then don't let others determine where your life should go. Believe in God and yourself and your dreams enough to not let others' opinions sway you from the road you have decided to travel. There will always be people who try to "warn" you of the imminent danger of your "bad" decision. Don't argue with them. Simply listen to what they say, look at it objectively to see if there is some truth you should heed, then discard the rest. People have comfort zones, and when you break away from their level of comfort, you upset them. Then they feel right in advising you of your mistake.

Growing up, you're going to hear and read a lot about goal setting. Most people see goals as targets that they aim for. You know where the target is, and you aim in that direction. Well, that's partially true. You do want to aim in the right direction. But you need to aim for something more than just aiming in the right direction. Aiming at a target is great for archery. But that falls short, too. If I'm serious about becoming a good marksman, I need to do more than just aim at a target. I need to aim for the bull's-eye on the target.

What most people don't know is that not every objective is a goal. So let's break this down. An **objective** is something you want. A **goal** is something you can do or accomplish **totally** by yourself. Everything else is a **desire**, because it involves the sometimes uncertain cooperation of another. Most of the things we want are desires. If I want to learn archery, which is a *desire*, first, I take lessons to learn how to use a bow and arrows. Someone else has to teach me what they know. Instead of having a private teacher, I could just buy a book or even go online to gain some instruction. The key is that *someone else is helping me* to get started with the basics. Once I have acquired the basic knowledge of handling the bow and aiming the arrow and taking precautions against self-inflicted injury by using the protective gear, then I am ready to start on the *goal* of developing accuracy. I can accomplish this on my own. The bull's-eye on my target is what I aim for. I do not just aim in the right direction. I can practice on my own and, with diligence, may turn out to be a rather good marksman.

It is important that you understand the difference between a goal and a desire. Study the diagram below.

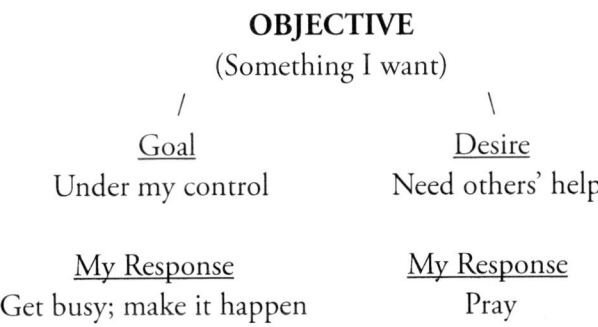

Below, I give an example so you can see how this works.

Objective:	I want to be an athlete when I grow up.
Goal(s):	I can find out which sports I'm good at.
	I can try out for school sports.
	I can try out for summer teams.
	I can practice whenever I can.
	I can give up video games, TV, etc., so I can **make time** to practice.
Desire(s):	I want to be the best athlete I can be.
	I want to be on my favorite team someday.

If you say you want something in the future, you have to start working on getting it right now. It will never come in the future if you don't start striving for it now. That's why it's important to start identifying your talents and abilities *now*. Some things won't be evident right away. They will unfold later. But there are things you can uncover and discover about yourself right now. Do you like to read or do you like numbers? Are you athletic, or could you sit for a long time and play checkers or chess? Do you make jokes a lot and like to hear people laugh, or are you more serious? Do you like to argue or do you try to help everyone get along? These are only some ideas to get you started thinking about who you are, what kind of person you are, and where you can go in life.

Your future life is another reason it's important to also know the difference between goals and desires. Once you have separated the two, then you can develop the right goals and work on those. Meanwhile, you pray for the desires. You pray that if your desires are in God's plan for your life, He will get you where He wants you to be.

Understanding the difference between goals and desires includes the ability to see that a stated goal may contain a goal *and* a desire. In the above example, I state my goal of trying out for school sports and summer teams. The true goal is that I try out. The outcome of my tryout is uncertain because someone other than me makes the call. I can't guarantee that I'll be on the teams. So that remains a desire.

ASPIRE

- **Blocked goals** will leave you **feeling angry or frustrated.**
- **Unreached goals** cause **anxiety, resentment, or guilt.**

Understanding and working on goals also includes understanding and accepting your own limitations. Contrary to what you might hear, we cannot do anything or everything we want to do. Sometimes we limit ourselves with fear and doubt, but sometimes there are very real limitations to what we can accomplish, no matter how hard we try.

When I wanted to be a concert pianist, I lacked the necessary information that would explain my limitations and why I would never even be a good pianist, much less a concert pianist. I learned much later, in my twenties, that because I wore splints I didn't crawl when I was a baby, so, I didn't develop eye/hand coordination. Simply put, I could recognize the keys on the piano. My eyes could read the music. But my hands couldn't do what was required without constantly looking at them, and then back to the music. This developmental lack also became apparent in a typing class during high school.

There was nothing I could do to change the way I had developed. It was a limitation. Just because I wasn't talented at playing the piano, that didn't mean I was not musically talented. I accepted that I was never going to excel at piano playing, so I turned to vocal music. God has given me a decent voice, and I worked on developing it. As I mentioned before, during high school I was in choirs all four years. I practiced our music at home so I could be better during class time. I memorized the music. I learned the right things to do in order to sing well. So, when one dream was never going to be realized, I adapted, and then developed the talent that I did have. Eventually, I took private voice lessons. I have sung in many choirs, ensembles, and I have done solos at church.

In reflecting on this limitation and being able to adapt, I wondered if it was something God did specifically to keep me off of the wrong path for my life. If God has a destiny for me that involves working with people and helping them grow, then being a concert pianist would not move me toward that destiny. Neither would being a talented typist.

God knew best the things I needed and didn't need in my life in order to move me toward His purposes for my life. When I understand and embrace these purposes, I can be secure, confident, and satisfied.

> "When you lose something in your life, stop thinking it's a loss for you . . . It is a gift you have been given so you can get on the right path to where you are meant to go, not to where you think you should have gone."
>
> ~ Suze Orman

> "I seldom think about my limitations, and they never make me sad. Perhaps there is just a touch of yearning at times; but it is vague, like a breeze among flowers."
>
> ~ Helen Keller

> "It is not because things are difficult that we do not dare, it is because we do not dare that they are difficult."
>
> ~ Lucius Annaeus Seneca

Nothing happens in your life without a reason. Sometimes the reason is simply because we're human and sometimes we make BIG, STUPID mistakes. But God is in control—even over our big, stupid mistakes. Nothing happens that He doesn't know about. Nothing happens that He doesn't allow. If He allows something bad, then even the bad has a purpose. I think my favorite Bible verse is Romans 8:28. It says, "And we know that ALL things work together for good, to those who LOVE God, to those who the called according to His purpose." ALL things. All hurts, all limitations, all deficiencies, all roadblocks, all trials, all crushed dreams, all injuries, all accidents, all tragedies, all good, all loving, all peaceful, all joyful . . . ALL. All things are for our good and God's glory. All things working together for good only applies to those who have trusted Jesus as their Savior and Lord and have been adopted into God's family.

Understanding your limitations doesn't mean giving up on all your dreams. It simply means you focus on the things you're good at and develop those as far as you can or want to go. Focus first on your strengths, abilities, and talents, while developing your character, and then, later on, you can always work on overcoming your limitations.

"The marvelous richness of human experience would lose something of rewarding joy if there were no limitations to overcome. The hilltop hour would not be half so wonderful if there were no dark valleys to traverse."

~ Helen Keller

Following are some questions for you to be able to discover who you are. Certainly, there is a lot more work to do in discovering who you are, but these questions can get you to start thinking. There are many books on these subjects. You will learn a lot about yourself if you read and apply what you read.

Who Are You?
- What is your birth order? Are you the firstborn, middle child, baby, or only child?
- How do you learn? Do you learn by hearing, seeing, touching, or doing?
- What are the things you're good at? Do you read fluently, or do you enjoy math? Do you have a natural sense of rhythm or exceptional musical ability? Do you have a love for science or can you easily decipher spatial components in a diagram? Do you understand yourself or do you understand others better?
  - » These are all multiple intelligences.
- How do you like to express love? How do you want others to express love to you?
  - » Do you like **Physical Touch**—hugs, pats on the back or head, taps on the shoulder?
  - » Do you like **Words of Affirmation**—words or written notes of encouragement, affirmation, and acceptance?

- » Do you like to spend **Quality Time** doing things together or just talking?
- » Do you like Receiving and **Giving Gifts**—feeling special when others give you gifts and presents?
- » Do you like others to do things for you —**Acts of Service**— like help you clean your room or make your favorite meal?
  - These are the five Love Languages.

- How do you like to be apologized to?
  - » Do you want the offender to **express regret**—by saying "I am sorry"?
  - » Do you want the offender to **accept responsibility**—by admitting "I was wrong"?
  - » Do you want the offender to **make restitution**—by offering "What can I do to make it right?"
  - » Do you want the offender to **express genuine repentance**— by saying "I'll try not to do that again"?
  - » Do you want the offender to **ask for forgiveness**—"Will you forgive me"?
    - These are the five Apology Languages.
- What things do you need to feel happy and content? These are your emotional needs. A list of emotional needs can be found in Talane Miedaner's book Coach Yourself to Success.

This chapter is on aspiring and becoming the best **you** can be. Does that mean you will be the best athlete, or musician, or artist, or whatever that the world has ever seen? No! There will always be someone better. It means that you learn what *you can do,* and then do it to the best of your abilities. Take lessons, practice, and work on getting better. Being the best at a career is of lesser importance. It is far more important to be a loving, gentle, self-controlled, empathetic person. Aspire to do better. Aspire to be better. Aspire to live better. Aspire to love better. Be the best YOU that you can be.

"To understand the heart and mind of a person, look not at what he has already achieved, but at what he aspires to."

~ Kahlil Gibran

"What happens to a man is less significant than what happens within him."

~ Louis L. Mann

"What lies behind us and what lies before us are tiny matters compared to what lies within us."

~ Henry David Thoreau

"If you don't learn from your mistakes, there's no sense making them."

~ Anonymous

"That first peak is the best place to pause and look back, to see if you took the easiest route, to learn the lessons from the first climb. And it is the best place to examine the terrain ahead, to change your plans and goals, to take a deep breath and begin climbing again."

~ Michael Johnson

"It is not our purpose to become each other; it is to recognize each other, to learn to see the other and honor him for what he is."

~ Hermann Hesse

"Life without a purpose is a languid, drifting thing; every day we ought to review our purpose, saying to ourselves, 'This day let me make a sound beginning.'"

~ Thomas Kempis

"A ship is safe in harbor, but that's not what ships are for."

~ William Shedd

"Happiness depends on ourselves."

~ Aristotle

3

Acquire

Acquire ~ verb
Definition:
1. To secure possession or control
2. To come to have

Acquire wise counsel.
~ Proverbs 1:5

The Challenge
Get all the information you can in school and in life in order to make your life the best it can be. Get the best education you can every year that you're in school. Ultimately, **you** *are responsible for your education. It may be difficult. Learning may be hard for you, but don't use that as an excuse not to learn at all. We all have subjects that we're good at, some we're not good at, some we love, and some we hate. Some subjects may seem irrelevant and unimportant. You may wonder why you have to take that particular class to get through school. Don't dismiss it, and then give up learning because you don't like it. Continue to try your best. Study more if you have to, get outside help to pass the class, and be confident that you gave it your best shot, even if your end grade is not an "A" or a "B."*

When you're done with your formal education, continue to seek out opportunities to learn. Life is full of wonderful adventures, exciting places, unique experiences, and interesting people. There are many, many things to get involved with—hobbies, sports, the arts, computers, gardening, cars and other vehicles, traveling, and much, much more. All of these things not only further your education, but they make you a well-rounded person. Also, acquire life skills in getting along with people.

Don't stop learning. You can learn something new every day. Acquire not only knowledge, but wisdom also.

I was an average kid academically. I didn't think I was smart, so I didn't try very hard. Some subjects I loved and did well in, and other subjects I disliked and did poorly in. Maybe that's you, right now. Maybe you're struggling with a subject that everyone says is important, but you just don't see it. You don't like the subject, don't do well in it, and just don't understand why you have to learn it. Right now, you don't see the importance of studying these subjects in school.

Maybe you have a passion for sports, theater or film, art or music, carpentry, welding, computers, or animals. Believe it or not, all of these things require at least a basic education, and some require a college education. Your education consists of things you hate as well as some things you love. In time, you will see that all of the undesirable subjects are important. It will definitely be better for you now if you accept that you need to learn subjects that hold no interest for you. Don't fight against it. Fighting against school, in general, and especially the subjects you don't like or don't feel you need, really only sets you up for further disappointment and failure. Fighting against it brings no gain or satisfaction to your life. There are other, more important battles to fight, so choose wisely.

Perhaps the beginning of your problems with a particular subject has to do with a teacher. Sometimes a teacher can say something to injure us, and then we develop a dislike toward the teacher, the class, or the subject. Most teachers don't intend to wound students with their comments, but maybe that is how you received it. So, look beyond your hurt, look beyond your assumption that the teacher is mean and doesn't like you. Look beyond your belief that a certain subject, or school, in general, is boring and try to understand that your education is your responsibility. You are there to learn, and you must do what is necessary in order for you to learn. **You create your reality.** You create a reality that is positive or you create a reality that is negative. For instance, you leave your home in a bad mood because your mother yelled at you. As you walk or ride the bus to school, someone teases you. This increases your anxiety, frustration, and anger. When you arrive at school, you run through the door and an adult reminds you of the school rules. You get angrier. In class, you tell the teacher you didn't do your homework. She won't listen to your reason and says this is a "no excuse environment" and that you'll have to stay in for recess to get it done. This makes you angrier. A few minutes later, a student bumps into you and you hit him. Now you're on your way to the principal's office. And you say you didn't do anything wrong? It is everyone else's fault. Really? Let's go back to the beginning. Maybe Mom had a good reason to yell at you, maybe she didn't. But you made the choice to be mad at your mom. From that point on, if someone even *looked* at you the wrong way, you thought the only response was to get angrier. But **you** made the choice to let the teasing bother you. **You** chose to run into the building and to see the adults as being mean to you. And **you** chose to hit the student who bumped you. Do you see how you created your reality? It all began with your choice to be mad at your mom. There were no choice corrections or attitude adjustments along the way, and so things just kept getting worse. Your trip to the principal's office is the consequence of a series of choices you made. Those choices kept you from learning. So, you were not being responsible for your education.

To say that it is everyone else's fault is being a victim. To have the attitude that your problems are a result of other people being against you . . . that is a victim mentality. To live life, especially when you are older, in a way that says "life just happens," is a sad existence and part of the victim mentality. We don't have to be victims. But it is the easy way out. If I'm a victim, then I don't have to try. If I'm a victim, I don't have to learn. If I'm a victim, I'm not responsible for anything. If I'm a victim, I don't have to respect anyone. If I'm a victim, I don't have to listen to anyone. If I'm a victim, people will feel sorry for me and won't expect or demand anything from me. Life can appear to be rather pleasant when I see myself as a victim. But the appearance is deceiving. Life is actually unpleasant. If I'm a victim, I depend on others for everything—**even my own happiness.** And I find myself never being happy. Truly, life just happens. Life happens **to** me, and I find myself not participating in my own life. And everything that happens will be bad and hurtful . . . because I'm a victim.

Victims don't get treated well. They don't get the breaks. As a victim, I have no dreams, no desires, no goals, nothing to offer in a job, so why should I work? When I'm a victim, I remain as a child emotionally. I don't develop emotional maturity because I see everything as being done *to* me or *for* me. So, why should I grow up? Developing emotional maturity is (in part) changing my perception and attitude from being a victim to being a victor. I don't mean victory in fighting, but rather victory internally—my thinking, my views, opinions, beliefs, preferences and convictions. Once I've changed my internal "stuff," I can then see all of life in a more positive way.

Can I make people like me? No. Whether someone likes me or not is their choice. Do I have to let their choice bother me? No. Moving out of the victim mentality requires me to understand the concept of choice, both others', and my own. Every person makes their own choices, and then is responsible for those choices. No one is responsible for another person's choice. Being responsible for my choice(s) is called *owning my choice*. Owning it simply means that I take ownership of the choices I make. I don't say, "He made me do it." I don't say, "Well, he hit me first." I simply say, "Yes, I did it," or "Yes, I said that."

Calling someone a name because they called me a name is reactive. Hitting someone because they hit me is reactive. Hitting someone because they called me a name is OVERreacting. Beating them up is OVERreacting. What they did (emotional hurt) doesn't deserve what I am giving back (physical hurt). Causing disruption in a classroom because I didn't get my way is OVERreacting. So, what can I do? I think, feel, and believe that they shouldn't have called me a name, hit me, tattled on me, stepped on my new shoes, cut in line, or taken my pencil. Because I think, feel, and believe I was wronged or hurt, I think, feel, and believe that they need to pay. They shouldn't be allowed to get away with it. Why is it wrong to want to hurt them back or make them pay?

It's wrong for many reasons. As a young person, you only know that you were hurt or wronged and you want justice or the other person to pay. You don't see the bigger picture. You don't know the reason behind the other person's choice to hurt you. They have a reason for what they did. It may not be a good reason, but it's their reason all the same. Maybe they were already in a very bad mood or were extremely sad. They didn't know how to get past their own feelings, and they hurt you. Then, when you react and hurt them back, the cycle continues and nothing **ever** gets better. Now, things are bad for you, and even worse for them. A person's sense of justice can be terribly slanted in favor of one's self, meaning EVERYONE is selfish and wants life to go their way. Dishing out our justice to others is unfair. We can take it too far.

This is why God says for you to let Him take care of the people who have wronged you. Only God knows how much retribution to dish out to each person. So don't play God and retaliate when someone wrongs you.

And don't tattle on others. Tattling serves three purposes. First, it's intended to get someone else in trouble. Second, it's intended to make the tattler look good. It builds up one while tearing down another. Third, it's intended to divert attention from the tattler's own wrongdoing to the other person's wrongdoing. Tattling is never a good way to solve your problems.

Are you perfect? Do you **always** listen and follow directions? Do you **always** obey the rules? Do you **always** do the right thing? Do you **always** get your homework done? Do you **always** speak well of **everyone**? Do you **always** go out of your way to help others? Do you **always** pick up after yourself? Do you **always** express gratitude and thankfulness, **never** complaining? Do you **always** appreciate what you have? Be honest. You may think you always do these things, but if any adult has to remind you of the rules or the expectations, correct you, tell you to watch your language, tell you to stop tattling, tell you to clean up your mess, tell you to stop complaining, tell you to stop arguing, tell you to stay out of other people's business . . . then you are not perfect. Only a perfect person can point the finger at someone else who does wrong.

So, what's a better way? A better way is **responding,** not reacting or overreacting, or tattling. Responding means I am in charge of my thoughts and choices and can take charge of my emotions. I must think of alternatives. I must think of what would be good for everyone. I must become proactive. I must think that the other person's choice was bad, but it didn't kill me. Then, I choose to not let the offense bother me. That doesn't mean that I bury my pain and move on. If I bury my pain, it will only surface at a later time. And it will be much worse. So, I deal with it now. Yes, it may hurt. I can't change the feeling that I get when the offense happens, *but what I do with those feelings and what I think about the person and what I want to do to the person who offended me is something I* **can** *change.* I can CHOOSE to change it. And, with God in my life, "I can do all things through Christ who strengthens me." I can choose to respond to them in kindness, gentleness, and understanding. I can choose to show mercy and grace to someone who has offended me.

"Whenever anyone has offended me, I try to raise my soul so high that the offense cannot reach it."

~ René Descartes

"To be wronged is nothing unless you continue to remember it."

~ Confucius

"No life is so hard that you can't make it easier by the way you take it."

~ Ellen Glasgow

"One who is injured ought not to return the injury, for on no account can it be right to do an injustice; and it is not right to return an injury, or to do evil to any man, however much we have suffered from him."

~ Socrates

"Anybody can become angry—that is easy, but to be angry with the right person and to the right degree and at the right time and for the right purpose, and in the right way—that is not within everybody's power and is not easy."

~ Aristotle

"How much more grievous are the consequences of anger than the causes of it."

~ Marcus Aurelius

"A quick-tempered man acts foolishly."

~ Proverbs 14:17a

"A hot-tempered man stirs up strife, but the slow to anger calms a dispute."

~ Proverbs 15:18

"This you know, my beloved brethren. But everyone must be quick to hear, slow to speak and slow to anger; for the anger of man does not achieve the righteousness of God."

~ James 1:19–20

Every choice affects our lives. Some are minor—like choosing what we are going to wear today. Others have more impact. Thoughts, choices, decisions, beliefs, convictions, and actions all contribute to make up who we are. Today, I am the person I am because of all the thoughts, doubts, questions, beliefs, decisions, convictions, and actions of all my previous days.

We live in a country that enjoys and champions free speech. Just because I don't like what someone says, he still has the right to say it. Was it hurtful? Maybe. Should he have said it? Probably not. But that's not the issue. *The issue is . . . What is my response going to be?* I cannot control what others say or do. I can only control myself, my choices, and my responses. I cannot change others. I can only work on changing myself. Others may use hurtful words and mean behavior as weapons against me. But I won't let others' words and actions turn my responses into weapons. What about you? Will you be a victim or a victor? Will you react or respond? Reacting takes no thought. Responding and being proactive requires much thought.

Too many times we go through school and can't wait to get out. We never want to sit in a classroom again. But, all of life is a classroom, an open door to learning. We have to learn how to manage our emotions. We need to learn about our bodies and how they can tell us when something is wrong. We have to learn how to manage our money. We need to learn about ourselves and other people and how we can have good, healthy relationships. The kind of person that continually learns is called a lifelong learner.

As you may have noticed, this chapter was NOT about acquiring fame, fortune, status, power, prestige, or a following on Twitter. It has been about acquiring an education, interests and hobbies, and gaining a well developed positive sense of identity. It is about securing possession or control of yourself by owning your choices and turning away from victim mentality. It has been about wisely picking your battles and seeing difficulty as an opportunity, rather than an obstacle. This one is hard for me, because all my life I have seen difficulty as an obstacle to get around, go through, go under, or over, not as an opportunity to grow or to do something out of the ordinary. Difficulty, whether it's a person or a problem, is intended to stretch us, to make us stronger, to prepare us for something even more difficult, much like stretching your muscles before a workout prepares your muscles for the workout.

In the last chapter, I encouraged you to not let naysayers deter and detour you from your passions and dreams. Now, I want to encourage you to follow the Proverbs 1:5 challenge to "acquire wise counsel." Wise counsel are those people you know who will not steer you in a wrong direction. They want to see you grow academically, emotionally, socially, physically, and spiritually. They really are looking out for your best interests, not their comfort zones. They want you to think for yourself and to take responsibility for your choices, but, they will give you many perspectives so that you can make an informed choice. They will not tell you what to do, nor will they heap guilt or shame on you when you make an unwise choice. They understand the importance of personal growth, applying yourself, being a victor, rather than a victim, responding rather than reacting. Their unspoken motto might be "live and learn" or "if at first you don't succeed, try, try again." Making your life the best it can be depends on proactively living your life, not reactively living with a victim mentality or letting life just happen.

> "Success is not to be measured by the position that one has reached in life, but the obstacles which he has overcome while trying to succeed."
>
> ~ Booker T. Washington

> "Intelligent people are always ready to learn. Their ears are open for knowledge."
>
> ~ Proverbs 18:15

> "Learning is not a spectator sport."
>
> ~ Anonymous

"Learning acquired in youth arrests the evil of old age; and if you understand that old age has wisdom for its food, you will so conduct yourself in youth that your old age will not lack for nourishment."

~ Leonardo da Vinci

"Learning is like rowing upstream, not to advance is to fall back."

~ Chinese Proverb

"He who asks a question may be a fool for five minutes, but he who never asks a question remains a fool forever."

~ Tom J. Connelly

"An education isn't how much you have committed to memory, or even how much you know. It's being able to differentiate between what you do know and what you don't."

~ Anatole France

"Education means inspiring someone's mind, not just filling their head."

~ Katie Lusk

"The principal goal of education is to create men who are capable of doing new things, not simply of repeating what other generations have done."

~ Jean Piaget, Swiss cognitive psychologist

"Learning never exhausts the mind."

~ Leonardo da Vinci

"Intellectual growth should commence at birth and cease only at death."

~ Albert Einstein

"Iron rusts from disuse; water loses its purity from stagnation . . . even so does inaction sap the vigour of the mind."

~ Leonardo da Vinci

"Very little is needed to make a happy life; it is all within yourself, in your way of thinking."

~ Marcus Aurelius

"Many people know so little about what is beyond their short range of experience. They look within themselves—and find nothing! Therefore they conclude that there is nothing outside themselves either."

~ Helen Keller

"The mind is not a vessel to be filled, but a fire to be kindled."

~ Plutarch

"Employ your time in improving yourself by other men's writings, so that you shall gain easily what others have labored hard for."

~ Socrates

"Knowledge that is seen to be controlled from the outside is acquired with reluctance, and it brings no joy."

~ Anonymous

"The happiness of your life depends upon the quality of your thoughts: therefore, guard accordingly, and take care that you entertain no notions unsuitable to virtue and reasonable nature."

~ Marcus Aurelius

"How could there be any question of acquiring or possessing, when the one thing needful for a man is to become—to be at last, and to die in the fullness of his being."

~ Antoine de Saint-Exupéry

4

Inquire

Inquire - verb
Definition:
1. To ask (a question)
2. To request information
3. A close examination
4. To make an investigation

The Challenge
Ask questions and question everything. All of life around us deserves our curiosity and further examination. Teachers in school teach the subjects the state says are important for students to learn. But, you can go beyond this notion and search out information on your own. Ask questions of everyone you know and meet. Take a small amount of information about something and request more information. Examine it further and investigate like you are Sherlock Holmes. If you attend a church that believes the Bible and you go to a public school, then question evolution when it's taught. It is still a theory, but it's taught like it's fact. Yes, you can question what is taught to you at school.

When I was very young, around five years of age, it seemed my favorite words were "How come?" Instead of asking "Why?" I asked "How come?" I asked "How come?" about EVERYTHING. I don't remember if I got good answers or not. Eventually, I stopped asking the "How come?" questions. I think I stopped asking questions altogether, at least while growing up.

In my adolescence or young adulthood, I developed and maintained a love for mysteries, crime, and sci-fi television shows and movies. Why? I love them because they address the unknown and the hard to understand. I love them because they ask questions, examine, and investigate. I love to try to solve the mystery or the crime before the people in the show can. I love using my thinking skills to take the clues and come up with the solution or to make connections that the characters in the story haven't made yet.

I am a deep thinker. In fact, I've been told I'm *too* deep. But this is one of my strengths—it's called intellection. I love discussing sci-fi programs that deal with time travel, alternate timelines, alternate dimensions, and the space-time continuum. Why? Because for me, it is fun. It is interesting to get other people's ideas, and then discuss them. It is interesting to compare my take on a particular program with the ideas someone else has on that same program. We agree on a lot, disagree on some, but always have a fun, thought-provoking discussion. Science is catching up to sci-fi, and what seemed impossible before, or what seemed like total fantasy, is now closer to happening in real life. By having discussions when it's still sci-fi, we can have a greater appreciation when it becomes real science.

I love discussing the hard questions of theology and philosophy, too. Why? Because discussing ideas and truths that are difficult or almost impossible to understand, keeps me thinking and growing. It keeps my brain active. And I can always learn a little more.

One way I learn more is to take a thought or a quote from someone and spend a while thinking about it and running it to the end as far as I can go and wherever it takes me. For instance, you may have heard the phrase, "Whatever doesn't kill you makes you stronger." Well, I thought about that and decided it's half true. It depends on what your idea of "stronger" is. Some individuals might believe stronger means the determination to get revenge or to be bitter and hurtful. Others, including me, think that stronger means not letting it defeat you; that you can rise above anything. If this is the correct meaning, then there's some necessary information that isn't given in this phrase. In order for something to make you stronger in a good way, you must **want** it to make you stronger. You must have a correct mind-set; a positive belief system; to trust that God is in control and will not let you be destroyed. Then, you will come through the problem stronger.

Another quote that intrigued me was "One must live the way one thinks, or end up thinking the way one has lived" ~ Paul Bourget. My thought progression came up with the following:

Living as one thinks requires examination of one's past and active participation in the making of one's future, to see tomorrow as a result of what one thinks and does today, to be aware of one's options and whatever subsequent choices that are made, and the ability to own those choices. Living as one thinks means living with intent and purpose.

Living as one thinks doesn't mean leaving God out of the picture. It means that as one is taking responsibility for and owning one's choices and behavior, one is actively partnering with God in the growth, healing, and maturing process. God does not heal, grow, mature, or sanctify without one's involvement. We cannot (and God cannot) change what is not acknowledged. One has to know and feel that one is wounded in order to find healing. One has to know that growth and maturity have not been attained in order to desire more. One has to know that one still sins in order to find grace, forgiveness, and further sanctification.

So, living as one thinks has many facets to explore.

Thinking as one has lived, on the other hand, means that somewhere in one's life stuff just happened. Purpose, drive, determination, ambition—all the qualities that propel a person from one day to the next—seem to vanish. A sense of victimization takes over, and instead of living life, one simply lets life happen—good, bad, ugly, indifferent—like today's storm, it'll pass—one hopes. For Christians, it's easy to become a "victim" of "God's will"; to have such a negative, fatalistic view of what God's will means, that one basically accepts anything and gives up on everything. There is a failure to accept one's own contribution and responsibility in every day of one's life. One has become a passive spectator in one's own life.

Thinking as one has lived can mean that one lived the best one could live with what one was willing to embrace. I think that's the key. If one is willing to embrace risk, responsibility, and ownership, then one will more likely live as one thinks. If one is not willing to embrace risk, responsibility, and ownership, then one will inevitably think as one has lived. Most likely, the life lived will be negative, judgmental, critical, legalistic, withdrawn, closed, joyless, hurt, angry, unforgiving, and self-pitying.

Thinking as one has lived means living a purposeless life. It means getting to the end of one's life, and after having lived such an empty life, one thinks exactly that way.

So, now you get an idea of how deep a thinker I am. What does all this have to do with inquiring? Well, I use questions to nudge me into the thinking process, questions I really don't even think about. Questions like "How are these two concepts different?" or "What's missing?" or "How can I develop that thought?" or "What did they really mean?" or "Can I take this idea and make it my own?" or "Can I come up with a way of explaining this to someone else?" or "How can I best interpret these concepts?" or "How does this apply to my life?" I became a detective with the concepts of living as one thinks and thinking as one lives. As I thought about them, the logic of their differences became apparent and a progression emerged. Once I gained a thorough and complete distinction between the two ideas, I had something that could make a difference in my life.

You may not want to do this much work in your life, but I challenge you to give it a try.

Sometimes we need to ask questions or examine things that seem to go wrong or badly. In eighth grade, I found myself in the middle of a conflict that I hadn't started. I was being accused of saying something that I didn't. I wasn't even able to give my side of it. I let the problem die down, but, for the remainder of the year, I wondered how the rumor got started. Then, I decided I was determined to figure it out, so I began replaying the scenario in my head. I examined it. I questioned it. How did this happen? Why was I being portrayed as spreading this information? Who really could have done it? Why would they have done it? As I played it out and asked the questions, a piece of information surfaced. I remembered there was a person sitting next to me on the bus who most likely heard the conversation and was responsible for starting the rumor. I never had the chance to confront this girl, so I never knew for sure if she was the culprit, nor the reasons why she would have started trouble. I had thought she was a friend. Over the years it became less important. But, figuring out how this conflict arose was enormously beneficial for my own peace of mind, even if there were several unanswered questions.

In the whole thinking process, there are several ways of reasoning—inductive, deductive, abductive, and retroductive. Abductive and retroductive are very hard concepts to understand, and I will not even attempt to explain them. That is something you can look into when you think you are ready. Inductive and deductive reasoning are a little easier to comprehend, especially if you see examples that illustrate how they work. Sherlock Holmes was famous for his deductive reasoning. He called it reasoning backward. In fact, here are a few of his criteria and quotes.

Do not theorize before gathering all the evidence.

"It is a capital mistake to theorize before you have all the evidence. It biases the judgment."

~ A Study in Scarlet

Do not reason or extrapolate from insufficient data.
"I had," he said, "come to an entirely erroneous conclusion, my dear Watson, how dangerous it always is to reason from insufficient data."

~ The Adventure of the Speckled Band

Consider the data or evidence.
"There is nothing like firsthand evidence."

~ A Study in Scarlet

Notice the small things or trifles.
"You know my method. It is founded upon the observation of trifles."

~ The Boscombe Valley Mystery

Look for deception in the obvious.
"There is nothing more deceptive than an obvious fact."

~ The Boscombe Valley Mystery

Don't just see, but really observe.
"The world is full of obvious things which nobody by any chance ever observes."

~ The Hound of the Baskervilles

Avoid feelings.
"The emotional qualities are antagonistic to clear reasoning."

~ The Sign of Four

Recognize incidental vs. vital facts
"It is of the highest importance in the art of detection to be able to recognize, out of a number of facts, which are incidental and which are vital. Otherwise your energy and attention must be dissipated instead of being concentrated."

~ The Reigate Puzzle

INQUIRE

Eliminate the impossible and what remains is the truth.
". . . when you have eliminated all which is impossible, then whatever remains, however improbable, must be the truth."

~ The Blanched Soldier

Deductive reasoning is top-down reasoning or logic. Deductive reasoning starts with a general piece of information and moves down to more specific details. You can also use it in pairs with the words "all and every," "no and don't," and with only the word "don't." Breaking them down to their basic forms looks like this:

Deductive Reasoning

1. All people breathe air
2. I am a person
3. I breathe air.

1. All babies cry
2. Every baby cries

1. No tables walk
2. Tables don't walk

1. Cats don't have fins
2. Siamese cats don't have fins
How do I know that Siamese cats don't have fins?
3. Because cats don't have fins

Inductive Reasoning

Inductive reasoning is bottom-up reasoning or logic. Induction starts with a specific piece of information and moves toward more general ideas.

1. Bob is a preacher
2. Most preachers read the Bible
3. Bob reads the Bible

1. Cleopatra was a Ptolemy
2. The Ptolemys ruled Egypt
3. Cleopatra ruled Egypt

"He who asks a question may be a fool for five minutes, but he who never asks a question remains a fool forever."

~ Tom J. Connelly

"To repeat what others have said requires education; to challenge it requires brains."

~ Mary Pettibone Poole

"Man's mind, once stretched by a new idea, never regains its original dimensions."

~ Oliver Wendell Holmes

"The important thing is not to stop questioning. Curiosity has its own reason for existing."

~ Albert Einstein

"Nothing has such power to broaden the mind as the ability to investigate systematically and truly all that comes under thy observation in life."

~ Marcus Aurelius

"The word 'why' not only taught me to ask, but also to think. And thinking has never hurt anyone. On the contrary, it does us all a world of good."

~ Anne Frank

"Questions can be like a lever you use to pry open the stuck lid on a paint can."

~ Fran Peavey

INQUIRE

"You can tell whether a man is clever by his answers. You can tell whether a man is wise by his questions."

~ Naguib Mahfouz

"We live in the world our questions create."

~ David Cooperrider

"Curiosity isn't the icing on the cake. It's the cake itself."

~ Susan Engel

"With a culture of questioning there is always more possibility."

~ Debra France, W. L. Gore

"A good question is never answered. It is not a bolt to be tightened into place but a seed to be planted and to bear more seed toward the hope of greening the landscape of idea."

~ John Anthony Ciardi

"We keep moving forward, opening new doors and doing new things, because we're curious, and curiosity keeps leading us down new paths."

~ Walt Disney

"The wise man doesn't give the right answers, he poses the right questions."

~ Claude Levi-Strauss

"Figuring out what you want to accomplish is a continual search—and questions are the means to the search."

~ Ron Shaich, CEO, Panera

"Judge a man by his questions rather than his answers."

~ Voltaire

"Questions are the engines of intellect, the cerebral machines which convert energy to motion, and curiosity to controlled inquiry."

~ David Hackett Fischer

"All education is about making people curious."

~ Stephen Sondheim

"If I had an hour to solve a problem and my life depended on the solution, I would spend the first 55 minutes determining the proper question to ask. For once I know the proper question, I could solve the problem in less than five minutes."

~ Albert Einstein

"The key to wisdom is this—constant and frequent questioning, for by doubting we are led to question and by questioning we arrive at the truth."

~ Pete Abelard

"As it is, the lover of inquiry must follow his beloved wherever it may lead him."

~ Plato, *Euthyphro*

"It is error only, and not truth, that shrinks from inquiry."

~ Thomas Paine

INQUIRE

"Science at its best is an open-minded method of inquiry, not a belief system."

~ Rupert Sheldrake

"Sometimes questions are more important than answers."

~ Nancy Willard

"He who has a why can endure any how."

~ Friedrich Nietzsche

"Questions are the creative acts of intelligence."

~ Anonymous

"Questioning is the door of knowledge."

~ Irish Saying

"There is no such thing as a worthless conversation, provided you know what to listen for. And questions are the breath of life for a conversation."

~ James Nathan Miller

5

Require

Require ~ verb
Definition:
1. To need
2. To insist upon: demand
3. To oblige: compel

The Challenge
Require more of yourself than to merely get by—require better thoughts, better attitudes, better beliefs, better speech, better behaviors/actions, better work.

Requiring more of yourself involves incorporating the challenges of admiring, aspiring, acquiring, and inquiring. You first must know qualities that you would like to build into your life. That is the "admiring." Then, you must aspire to be the best you can be. Then, you must acquire a "lifelong learner" mentality, where you see everything as an opportunity to learn. Then, you must inquire about everything, and keep inquiring—never stop. Now, you are equipped with the tools to go to the next level, that of requiring more of yourself. To require more of yourself is to insist upon or demand a stretching of yourself in different areas of your life, like stretching your body before you exercise. We aren't stretched by difficulty only. We can choose to stretch or require more of ourselves in order to solve a problem, mend a relationship, complete an assignment by a deadline, or any other seemingly monumental task. To require more of yourself is to push yourself a little harder when you feel like giving up. Requiring more of yourself means that you strive for excellence in all that you do—not perfection, but excellence.

I did not require much of myself growing up. I did what I was told . . . in school, at home, and at church. Others required certain things of me, and that's what I did—no more, no less. I didn't see adults requiring much of themselves, so I followed their lead. No one ever addressed the idea of requiring more of yourself or of pursuing excellence. Oh, perfection was expected of me, but not excellence.

Where and how does excellence begin? How will you know when you are and aren't pursuing excellence? The answer is in a quote.

"Excellence is an art won by training and habituation. We do not act rightly because we have virtue or excellence, but we rather have those because we have acted rightly.

"We are what we repeatedly do. Excellence, then, is not an act, but a habit."

~ Aristotle

Excellence is not *one thing* that we did today. It is an *accumulation* of things we have done excellently and repeatedly—today, yesterday, last week, last month, and so on. It is the best choices we could possibly make. Even when we don't feel good, or we're angry or hurt, we can still choose to pursue excellence instead of mediocrity. When we habitually do things in an excellent way, meaning, we have made excellence a habit, then the habit becomes a lifestyle. The same applies to mediocrity. Too many people choose to live at a mediocre level. Once we are okay with mediocrity, it becomes our comfort zone, and then a rut. Then, the rut is almost impossible to get out of.

Intentionally choose excellence over mediocrity every day. If nothing else, you will know that you did your personal best. Below is a contrast of excellence and perfection. I don't know who wrote it, but I think this is a very good definition of both.

>Excellence is willing to be wrong,
>>Perfection is being right.
>Excellence is risk,
>>Perfection is fear.
>Excellence is powerful,
>>Perfection is anger and frustration.
>Excellence is spontaneous,
>>Perfection is control.
>Excellence is accepting,
>>Perfection is judgment.
>Excellence is giving,
>>Perfection is taking.
>Excellence is confident,
>>Perfection is doubt.
>Excellence is flowing,
>>Perfection is pressure.
>Excellence is journey,
>>Perfection is destination.

"Excellence is to do a common thing in an uncommon way."

~ Booker T. Washington

"I would rather excel in the knowledge of what is excellent, than in the extent of my power and possessions."

~ Plutarch

"I count him braver who overcomes his desires than him who conquers his enemies; for the hardest victory is over self."

~ Aristotle

REQUIRE

Require Better Thoughts—

It is so easy to let our thoughts be negative, judgmental, critical, and undermining to ourselves as well as toward others. The Bible says that as we think, so we are. Our thoughts determine what kind of people we become.

If my thoughts are on getting even with someone for something they did to me, then I will become a vengeful, bitter, and manipulative person. If I think about the hardships of others and want to help them, then I become empathetic, and my desire to serve and help others deepens. If I complain and gripe about my life, then I will become a grown-up complainer. If I constantly want to get out of doing things (chores, schoolwork, etc.), then I will be a slacker. If I find things to enjoy and find wonderment in life, then I will be a pleasant, grateful adult. If I see myself as being put here for a noble purpose, then I will often see doors of opportunity. If I see myself as being a misfit, too fat or skinny, too short or tall, a nerd or a geek, or the awkward, clumsy one, then I will continue to see myself that way in years to come.

"A man's as miserable as he thinks he is."

~ Lucius Annaeus Seneca

"Finally, brethren, whatever is true, whatever is honorable, whatever is right, whatever is pure, whatever is lovely, whatever is of good repute, if there is any excellence and if anything worthy of praise, dwell on these things."

~ Philippians 4:8

"Why should we think upon things that are lovely? Because thinking determines life. It is a common habit to blame life upon the environment. Environment modifies life but does not govern life. The soul is stronger than its surroundings."

~ William James

"Man can alter his life by altering his thinking."

~ William James

"Once I realized that right thinking is vital to victorious living, I got more serious about thinking about what I was thinking about, and choosing my thoughts carefully."

~ Joyce Meyer

"The most common way people give up their power is by thinking they don't have any."

~ Alice Walker

"The secret of living a life of excellence is merely a matter of thinking thoughts of excellence. Really, it's a matter of programming our minds with the kind of information that will set us free."

~ Charles R. Swindoll

Require a Better Attitude—
A lot of people think that attitude is tied to emotions. If I am angry, my attitude will be defensive and confrontational. If I am hurt or sad, my attitude will be "It doesn't matter," or "I don't care," or "Poor me." While we can't change the initial emotion when it happens, we can choose to not let the emotions rule and dictate what happens next. We can change our attitude so that we get along with others, rather than making life miserable for others. You have a right to feel what you feel. You just don't have the right to force everyone around you to endure your tantrums and tirades.

However, though it is influenced by your emotions, attitude is more directly tied to and affected by your thoughts. Attitude is a result of what your thoughts are about what you're feeling. As you practice thinking better thoughts, your attitude will improve.

"The only difference between a good day and a bad day is your attitude."

~ Dennis S. Brown

"Attitude is a little thing that makes a big difference."

~ Winston Churchill

"He who has so little knowledge of human nature as to seek happiness by changing anything but his own disposition will waste his life in fruitless efforts."

~ Samuel Johnson

Require Better Beliefs—
What do you believe about yourself, life, women, men, your future, your work/career, dreams, destiny, God? As children, we believe what most people tell us. We believe what the teachers teach us at school. We believe what our parents or guardians tell us. Eventually, some of what was taught and told to us may one day need to be corrected.

But, sometimes other beliefs take hold that no one ever taught us. I'm talking about a belief that takes root because of a deep emotional wound combined with a fear.

When I was young, my father severely disappointed me on one specific occasion. He took me to a piano lesson, and then left. He was supposed to be there to take me back home, but a taxi took me home instead. I felt abandoned. Then, a fear took hold, the fear that no one had the money to pay the cabdriver. And then a belief took root. I began to believe that every time there was an unforeseen expense, that I would never have enough money. This belief on a subconscious level ruled my life for forty-some years. My life actually produced what I feared and believed. I was a slave to the fear and belief that I would never have enough money, especially in times of emergency. This fear and belief also blocked truths from the Bible so that they never reached into my heart, which was the main reason I was always so pessimistic. Truth remained locked somewhere in my mind, but could not penetrate the weeds of deception already planted there. I was double minded. I believed what I knew of God, but I also believed the fear and the other powerfully deceptive belief.

In recent years, praying for my financial needs to be met, repenting of bad financial decisions and wrong choices, and trying to commit to the discipline of tithing, never worked—and I could never figure out why.

When I was confronted with the idea that I was fearful (about accumulating more debt), it brought to mind the memory of my disappointment, and the belief that I had lived by for so long. I did the work required in order to gain freedom from this fear and belief. I repented of the right thing—the root of my financial problem. I can now say that I live by a new belief, and that joy, contentment, a spirit of giving, and envisioning a great and powerful God who wants to do great and powerful things are the fruit of my new root. When you change (or destroy) the root, you can change the fruit.

"The naïve believes everything, but the sensible man considers his steps."

~ Proverbs 14:15

Require Better Speech—

Though I'm a stickler for correct English grammar, the better speech I am referring to is not grammar. I am talking about clean vocabulary. Just because most of the people around you may use profanity, and TV shows and movies use profanity . . . that does not mean that you should be using it. When I was young it was said that only uneducated people used profanity. Unfortunately, now, even the most educated people use the worst possible language.

If you are going to pursue excellence, you must rise above the mediocrity of foul language. Cursing at people and things **really means you are speaking a curse against them or it.** If you want a prosperous life, then don't curse everything around you. Learn to bless instead. There are many words that you can use to convey the meaning of something without lowering yourself to profanity. This is an excellent way for you to increase your vocabulary, too.

If you have already started using obscenities, it may be difficult to stop, but you can do it. Just remember, you're striving for excellence and you are requiring more of yourself.

Striving for better speech also includes no name-calling, lying, or deceptions.

"When there are many words, transgression is unavoidable, but he who restrains his lips is wise."

~ Proverbs 10:19

"He who speaks truth tells what is right, but a false witness, deceit."

"There is one who speaks rashly like the thrusts of a sword, but the tongue of the wise brings healing."

"Truthful lips will be established forever, but a lying tongue is only for a moment."

~ Proverbs 12:17–19

"The one who guards his mouth preserves his life, the one who opens wide his lips comes to ruin."

~ Proverbs 13:3

"A truthful witness saves lives, but he who utters lies is treacherous."

~ Proverbs 14:25

"Whenever the speech is corrupted, so is the mind."

~ Lucius Annaeus Seneca

"Let no unwholesome word proceed from your mouth . . ."

~ Ephesians 4:29

". . . and there must be no filthiness and silly talk, or coarse jesting, which are not fitting, but rather giving of thanks."

~ Ephesians 5:4

Require Better Behavior/Actions—

This is all about what you do moment by moment. Your actions are a result of your thoughts, attitudes, and beliefs, and often include what you feel you need or are not getting. If your thoughts are "I know I'm bad because everybody says I'm bad," or "Why should I try? Nobody likes what I do," or "I'll never measure up," or "This is too hard, so why bother?" or "I'm just a problem to everyone," or "I must be broken because my mom says I am," or "I want/need something, but I know I won't get it," or other negative thoughts, then your attitude will follow. Your expectations of yourself will be low, and your expectations of others will be either that they'll hurt you like you've been hurt already, or that **they** will raise you up to a high level. Most likely, your expectation will be that they will hurt you, reject you, neglect you, or abandon you. So, with all this going on in your head, it's only logical that your behavior would reflect it.

Besides your own thoughts and attitudes producing your behavior, there is another way your behavior is formed. It's the behavior you see from just about everyone around you. If adult family members or friends throw things when they're angry, then you'll think that's how you can express anger. You'll see nothing wrong with it because "everybody does it."

This is where you can choose to be different—to require better of yourself. It can be done. You can be the leader, not the follower. Change it now before it becomes habitual and you grow up with the same problem areas you see in those around you. Find people you can talk to about your hurts and your anger. Learn when you can express it and when it's not appropriate to express it. You always want to acknowledge the pain and/or anger, but you don't always have to express it or act on it. Acknowledging and expressing are two different things.

I have found that the outbursts of anger that I had as an adult were rooted in my childhood. As a child, I could never express any of my feelings—not to anyone—and they stayed bottled up. I didn't know how to simply acknowledge them either. Then, they got covered up with years of additional pain, all the while becoming fiercer. Sometimes I would blow up like a volcano. But that was only some of it. There was more—way more. It took the death of someone close to me for me to figure out where my anger came from. Once I figured it out, I dealt with the pain by giving myself the voice I never had. I sorted it all out with God and grieved. Not long after, I noticed that I was not yelling in anger anymore. I had mellowed considerably.

"Be angry and yet do not sin, do not let the sun go down on your anger."

~ Ephesians 4:26

"Let your light shine before men in such a way that they may see your good works, and glorify your Father who is in heaven."

~ Matthew 5:16

"When you do the common things in life in an uncommon way, you will command the attention of the world."

~ George Washington Carver

"I have been impressed with the urgency of doing. Knowing is not enough; we must apply. Being willing is not enough; we must do."

~ Leonardo da Vinci

Require Better Work—

Requiring better work of yourself does not refer only to the physical output that you do. As in just about everything I've presented here, better work begins in your mind. You can only produce better work, whether physical, intellectual, or emotional, by producing better thoughts. That's why "work" is the last one on the list.

We've all heard "practice makes perfect." I grew up with this phrase. But, at some point in my life, I realized that it is not true. Practice makes permanent. So, if you are making an error somewhere, the more you practice, the more permanent the error will be. You must correct the error, and then practice, practice, practice.

In my piano lessons, my practicing never produced perfect results. I would make a mistake, stop, say "wait," and try again, only to find myself making the same mistake and repeating the same ritual, over and over. I became perfect at practicing the problem area. No one ever stopped to show me how I might get off of my practice treadmill, probably because no one knew how, and, to my knowledge, everyone believed that practice made perfect.

Work, or labor, is something that we all have to do. It's important that we develop the right thoughts and attitudes concerning the work we are given or the work we choose to do. It should always be seen as a gift from God, a blessing, and should be performed to the best of our abilities and in worship to God. I will go into more detail in the next chapter.

> "Furthermore, as for every man to whom God has given riches and wealth, He has also empowered him to eat from them and to receive his reward and rejoice in his labor; this is the gift of God."
>
> ~ Ecclesiastes 5:19

> "With good will render service, as to the Lord, and not to men."
>
> ~ Ephesians 6:7

REQUIRE

"No individual has any right to come into the world and go out of it without leaving behind him distinct and legitimate reasons for having passed through it."

~ George Washington Carver

In all six of these areas—thoughts, attitudes, beliefs, speech, actions, and work—you are able to choose. You are able to choose what, when, where, why, and how. **Learn now** that the power to choose is yours **right now**. You don't have to wait to be an adult to know that you have the power over your thoughts, attitudes, beliefs, speech, actions, and work. The sooner you take charge of these areas and learn better, more positive ways, the better your life will be as an adult. If you continue to let the garbage of life—anger, hurt, bitterness, fear, pride, and selfishness—rule your existence, then, it will be much harder for you as an adult. Not only will you have to deal with so much negativity in your life, you will also have to repent of and unlearn all the garbage that you thought was so important. Life is too short to waste your youth on being angry, hurt, hostile, and no fun to be around.

"The mind unlearns with difficulty what it has long learned."

~ Lucius Annaeus Seneca

6

Perspire

Perspire ~ verb
Definition:
To excrete perspiration

The Challenge
Work hard in everything you set out to do. Put 100 percent of yourself in every task, chore, project, assignment, job, talent, and passion given to you by others or God.

Work hard at putting your life in order.

Work hard at being the kind of person employers want on their team.

Work hard at being a wife and mother or husband and father.

In my challenge, working hard in most of these areas will not literally produce perspiration. Some might. Let's take a look at working hard in a specific sport.

I'm not into playing sports, but I have enjoyed watching certain teams. When Michael Jordan was on the Bulls, I watched a lot of games. He was an extraordinary player—a true team player, not a one-man hotdogger. He put everything he had into each game. He sweated. He required much of himself in order to produce a winning team, both as a player and as captain. I would recommend that you find old video footage and watch his games.

Looking back on my life, I can say I hardly ever worked very hard. I didn't work hard on my grades in school. I didn't work terribly hard around the house. There were times when I gave my all, but those were the things I liked doing. I remember in my junior year of high school, the a cappella choir was doing a spring operetta. I signed up for set design and construction as well as performing. We worked on the set after school till very late, every day, till just before performance time. I loved doing that, and I put a great deal of time and energy into it. I also loved singing and gave it the very best I could.

As far as my adult life goes, oh, there were plenty of hard jobs—it's just that I didn't put my "all" into them. I guess my philosophy was . . . If I don't like doing something, then I'm not going to put 100 percent effort into it. I didn't **require** enough of myself to put in the energy and effort to accomplish the task assigned to me. Oh, I completed the assigned task. But, could I have put more into it? Of course, I could have. I could have, and should have, learned from Joseph the dreamer about how to do a job.

In the Bible, Joseph, the son of Jacob, had dreams given to him by God. They were dreams that told him his future—BUT, only the good part. His dreams were of people bowing down to him because he was important. Then, his life seemed to take a turn for the worse. His brothers wanted to kill him, but decided to sell him into slavery instead.

He is taken from his home and homeland, and ends up in Egypt. Here, he serves a man named Potiphar. Joseph puts 100 percent of himself into serving this man. Potiphar is blessed because of Joseph's work, and he makes Joseph head of all his household. Now, he is still a slave, but he has been given great responsibility. He still gives 100 percent of himself. This lasts for a while. Then he has a false accusation made against him, and he is thrown in jail.

He is in jail for a while. He works while he's there, and the jailor is blessed because of Joseph's work. Then two of Pharaoh's servants land in jail. They have dreams that Joseph interprets for them. One dreams of being restored to his place of service, the other dreams of himself being killed. The men are released from jail, and things unfold just as Joseph said they would. Joseph continues to work hard during his imprisonment. The jailor rewards him with greater responsibility. Eventually, Pharaoh has some strange dreams, and he is told that Joseph, a man in jail, can interpret dreams. Pharaoh has Joseph brought before him. Pharaoh tells Joseph the dreams, and Joseph interprets them. Pharaoh is impressed with not only the interpretation, but with Joseph's wisdom concerning the coming disaster. Pharaoh elevates Joseph to second in command.

The story of Joseph is not meant to imply that if we work hard, then we will one day rule a country. It simply means that when we do our jobs with the right motivation and give all we can give, then we can live with a clear conscience. What was Joseph's motivation? It wasn't to rule a country. It was simply to honor God. He trusted that God was taking care of him in all the dark and lonely places, and he worked in slavery "as unto the Lord."

There is a prevalent mind-set today that is quite disturbing. It is that some young employees are not fulfilling the responsibilities of the positions they hold. These young employees stand around talking to each other and ignore the paying customers. They seem to feel that **they** should get paid a good wage for doing absolutely nothing, when, in actuality, these young employees are damaging the businesses they work for. How are they damaging them? When customers are not helped and made to feel unwelcome at a business, those same customers go home and tell family and friends about the rude and unprofessional behavior they witnessed and received. Word gets around, and soon the business is losing a lot of customers or clients. A business or company is in business to sell a product or service and to make a profit. If employees do not have the desire to help the business stay in business, then they are working against their employers. Eventually, the employee is let go for any number of reasons, and unfortunately, the closing of the business might follow.

Here is an interesting idea to ponder. When you get a job, work at that job for the betterment and advancement of the business/company. You are being hired to do a job for that business—not to advance yourself. Most businesses want to see you advance and will work with you to help you do that. But, you have to show them that you're worth the investment. And you do this by working to prosper them.

I think this idea is seen in the life and work of Joseph. His main objective was to honor God. He worked as if God alone was his boss, and he worked to build up the worth of those he worked for. God blessed Joseph, and He blessed those who "employed" Joseph.

For some reason, we tend to think that the hard job, the unwanted assignment, or the poor working conditions are beneath us. We want life to be good, prosperous, comfortable, and easy. But, nothing in life **ever** comes easy. If you want to be good at playing an instrument, playing a sport, singing, acting, painting/drawing/sculpting, reading, math, science, etc., you have to work at it. You have to put forth the effort to study, learn, practice, and then keep studying, keep learning, and keep practicing. If you want to be able to land a job, then give it, and your employers, the best that you can. Work in your position as if the business depended on you—because, in a way, it does. Own whatever position you have, give it 100 percent, and the best that you have to give.

Perspiring is not only about giving your all in a job. In the challenge, I also encourage you to work hard at putting your life in order, and also, work hard at being a good spouse and parent. It is wise to begin looking at problem areas of your life and to begin correcting them now. I have addressed many things that either I have experienced or have seen in others. To put your life in order and to be the kind of adult who has good relationships, and to be a good spouse and parent, you must grow emotionally as you age chronologically. Emotional growth and maturity doesn't just automatically happen when you become a certain age (i.e., sixteen, eighteen, twenty-one, or whatever age you believe is the "magic" age). I know from experience that you can be stuck emotionally at a young age. The way you react (rather than respond) to hurts, issues, etc., is a clue about where you are stuck. To move yourself in the direction of emotional growth, you must be healed of certain painful experiences and memories. You must be courageous enough to feel the pain again, with the intention of healing and forgiving the offender(s). You never want to relive the pain simply to continue feeling miserable, or to become angrier and bitter. Lack of emotional maturity affects every area of life, including spiritual growth.

MOVE YOURSELF, MOVE THE WORLD

You may or may not have dreams of being married and having children. If you do, please understand that there is no reason why you can't have a good, healthy marriage and family. It takes two emotionally healthy adults to have both the good marriage and family. One person in the marriage **can** do it alone, but it is much, much harder. There is so much information out there on developing yourself, your marriage, and your family, that there really is no excuse for staying unhealthy and undeveloped. At that point, it simply is a matter of being stubborn and strong willed, and not wanting to change. I encourage you to be brave and unafraid, to leave stubbornness behind, to embrace change, and move past your comfort zones.

> "We all have a path to take; sometimes it's hidden under the weeds, so you might have to work a little."
>
> ~ Mike Dolan, www.hawaiianlife.com

> "Even if you're on the right track, you'll get run over if you just sit there."
>
> ~ Will Rogers

> "Hard work spotlights the character of people: some turn up their sleeves, some turn up their noses, and some don't turn up at all."
>
> ~ Sam Ewig

> "The price of success is hard work, dedication to the job at hand, and the determination that whether we win or lose, we have applied the best of ourselves to the task at hand."
>
> ~ Vince Lombardi

> "I always wanted to be the best I could be at whatever I did. I didn't want to be the number one golfer in the world, I just wanted to be as good as I could be. I work hard, I push myself hard, and I probably even expect too much of myself."
>
> ~ Greg Norman

PERSPIRE

"Nothing of great value in this life comes easily. The things of highest value sometimes come hard. The gold that has the greatest value lies deepest in the earth, as do the diamonds."

~ Norman Vincent Peale

"You have to put in many, many, many tiny efforts that nobody sees or appreciates before you achieve anything worthwhile."

~ Brian Tracy

"I focus on my work. If I let myself get distracted by the insults and slanders I wouldn't get anything substantive done."

~ Norman Finkelstein

"Long shots do come in and hard work, dedication and perseverance will overcome almost any prejudice and open almost any door."

~ John H. Johnson

"If the boss is a jerk, get over it. First of all, don't you think that there's a good chance that your boss's boss knows what's going on? If so, just keep your head down and do the work. Usually, if you put in maximum effort and produce excellent results, someone in the company is going to take notice. Either you will get promoted or your jerky boss will get the heave-ho. It happens all the time."

~ Suze Orman

"I do not think that there is any other quality so essential to success of any kind as the quality of perseverance. It overcomes almost everything, even nature."

~ John D. Rockefeller

"My belief is firm in a law of compensation. The true rewards are ever in proportion to the labor and sacrifices made . . ."

~ Nikola Tesla

"Try not to become a man of success. Rather, become a man of value."

~ Albert Einstein

"Give me six hours to chop down a tree and I will spend the first four sharpening the axe."

~ Abraham Lincoln

"Lazy hands make a man poor, but diligent hands bring wealth."

~ Proverbs 10:4

"He who works his land will have abundant food, but he who chases fantasies lacks judgment."

~ Proverbs 12:11

"The lazy man does not roast his game, but the diligent man prizes his possessions."

~ Proverbs 12:27

"The sluggard craves and gets nothing, but the desires of the diligent are fully satisfied."

~ Proverbs 13:4

"All hard work brings a profit, but mere talk leads only to poverty."

~ Proverbs 14:23

PERSPIRE

"The laborer's appetite works for him; his hunger drives him on."

~ Proverbs 16:26

"What one has, one ought to use; and whatever he does he should do with all his might."

~Marcus Tullius Cicero

"Shun no toil to make yourself remarkable by some talent or other . . ."

~ Lucius Annaeus Seneca

"About the only thing that comes to us without effort is old age."

~ Gloria Pitzer

"It's not about perfect. It's about effort. And when you bring that effort every single day, that's where transformation happens. That's how change occurs."

~ Anonymous

"Look at a day when you are supremely satisfied at the end. It's not a day when you lounge around doing nothing; it's when you've had everything to do and you've done it."

~ Margaret Thatcher

"The heights by great men reached and kept,
Were not attained by sudden flight,
But they, while their companions slept,
Were toiling upward in the night."

~ Henry Wadsworth Longfellow

"God gave us two ends—one to sit on and one to think with. Success depends on which one you use. Head you win, tail you lose."

~ Anonymous

"The person who is waiting for something to turn up might start with their shirt sleeves."

~ Garth Henrichs

"He who would learn to fly one day must first learn to stand and walk and run, climb and dance; one cannot fly into flying."

~ Friedrich Nietzsche

"No one ever drowned in his own sweat."

~ Ann Landers

"Some people dream of success . . . while others wake up and work hard at it."

~ Anonymous

"At the end of the day, you are solely responsible for your success and your failure. And the sooner you realize that, you accept that, and integrate that into your work ethic, you will start being successful. As long as you blame others for the reason you aren't where you want to be, you will always be a failure."

~ Erin Cummings

"The difference between try and triumph is a little umph."

~ Anonymous

PERSPIRE

"Many an opportunity is lost because a man is out looking for four-leaf clovers."

~ Anonymous

"Labor disgraces no man; unfortunately, you occasionally find men who disgrace labor."

~ Ulysses S. Grant

"It is surprising what a man can do when he has to, and how little most men will do when they don't have to."

~ Walter Linn

"Plough deep while sluggards sleep."

~ Benjamin Franklin

"You cannot plough a field by turning it over in your mind."

~ Anonymous

"God gives every bird its food, but He does not throw it into its nest."

~ J. G. Holland

"All the so-called secrets of success will not work unless you do."

~ Anonymous

7

Inspire

Inspire ~ verb
Definition:
1. To guide or affect by divine influence
2. To fill with high emotion: exalt
3. To stimulate to creativity or action
4. To elicit: arouse

The Challenge
As you reach adulthood and you have admired, aspired, acquired, inquired, required, and perspired, then the last thing for you to do is to inspire. At this point, you have become a person with good, positive character qualities. You have aspired to find out who you are as God made you, the talents and abilities He has given you, and you have dreamed a dream of your contribution to the world. You secured possession of an identity known as "lifelong learner," and hopefully, you have acquired wisdom as well. You have developed curiosity and have inquired about everything. You have required a high standard for yourself, and learned to have self-control and discipline. Finally, you have perspired; working long hours to finish homework assignments, projects, term papers, plus working one or two part-time jobs while still helping around the house.

INSPIRE

Now, it is time to inspire the younger ones that may be admiring you.

Now, with all that you have gained, you are equipped with the essentials and can pass these on to the young people around you. When you desire to inspire others, you desire a good thing. We all need to see or hear that someone rose above their hardships and did well in life. Those are inspiring stories.

This was the hardest chapter to write, because there didn't seem to be much to say on the idea of inspiring others. Then, I looked at some quotes I had gathered, and it hit me. Inspiring really is about leading or influencing. If someone inspired you—they led you. They led or influenced your thinking. They led or influenced your behavior and actions. They may have led or influenced you in your choice of job or career. But, remember, inspiring is an **uplifting and positive** action. Everyone leads and influences others, whether we know it or not. Sometimes, though, it's a negative or dangerous influence. We have looked at some of those in previous chapters. You don't have to let those negative influences become part of your life or keep you down. Look to others of good character and good deeds to find your inspiration. And we are back full circle to the beginning—Admire. When you look for and find people to admire, you become inspired. If you have taken the words and ideas of this book seriously, and have worked on making yourself a better person, then hopefully, I have *inspired* you.

"If your actions inspire others to dream more, learn more, do more and become more, you are a leader."

~ John Quincy Adams

"Everyone's life is an object lesson to others."

~ Karl G. Maeser

"You can really change the world if you care enough."

~ Marion Wright Edelman

MOVE YOURSELF, MOVE THE WORLD

"Each time someone stands up for an ideal, or acts to improve the lot of others, or strikes out against injustice, he sends forth a tiny ripple of hope."

~ Robert F. Kennedy

"The pessimist complains about the wind. The optimist expects it to change. The leader adjusts the sails."

~ John Maxwell

"The greatest good you can do for another is not just share your riches, but reveal to them their own."

~ Benjamin Disraeli

"The test we must set for ourselves is not to march alone but to march in such a way that others will wish to join us."

~ Hubert Humphrey, U.S. vice president, senator

"He that would be a leader must be a bridge."

~ Welsh Proverb

"The question should be, is it worth trying to do, not, can it be done."

~ Allard Lowenstein, twentieth-century American diplomat

"The best leader brings out the best in those he has stewardship over."

~ J. Richard Clarke

"Example sheds a genial ray which men are apt to borrow, So first improve yourself today, and then your friends tomorrow."

~ Anonymous

INSPIRE

In this book, I have given you something that I did not have growing up. Oh, I had the Bible and was taught many good and valuable lessons. I just never had anyone use only a few simple verbs to express a better way of being and living, or to teach me ways of dealing with emotional wounds and getting along with others. In my youth, I don't recall that sermons or Bible studies addressed acquiring skills for relationships, or of pursuing excellence, or of working hard and putting your all into something. The Bible does address all three. But I only remember being taught theology and doctrine. At a young age, I became very grounded in my faith, but growing up, there seemed to be a lack of important information about *how* to grow up and be a responsible adult. Even just two of these words could have changed my **outlook** as a child, and put my life on a different level.

This is what I share with you in these pages—that you have seven words—admire, aspire, acquire, inquire, require, perspire and inspire— that can help you to change **your outlook on life**. May these words and chapters awaken you to the choices available, the need to work hard, understand people and situations, and to give back.

"We should be taught not to wait for inspiration to start a thing. Action always generates inspiration. Inspiration seldom generates action."

~ Frank Tibolt

"It is difficult to inspire others to accomplish what you haven't been willing to try."

~ Anonymous

"For once you have tasted flight you will walk the earth with your eyes turned skywards, for there you have been and there you will long to return."

~ Leonardo da Vinci

MOVE YOURSELF, MOVE THE WORLD

"You will be as much value to others as you have been to yourself."

~ Marcus Tullius Cicero

"Life well spent is long."

~ Leonardo da Vinci

"The high destiny of the individual is to serve rather than to rule."

~ Albert Einstein

In all the pages of this book, I have set before you ideas on how to become the person God intended you to be. I would be remiss in my responsibility if I did not add something in this final part. Though these seven words, properly applied and worked on throughout life, can be change agents for a better you, these words alone miss something that is of utter importance. You see, though working on these aspects of life may bring improvement and empowerment, they touch only a small part of your life—the part that thinks, plans, and makes choices. Your heart is left unchallenged and unchanged. The heart is the seat of affections. Only when your heart has been turned to God will you be truly changed. These seven words can have a phenomenal impact on your life when your heart has been changed because your spirit has been reborn. Spiritual rebirth comes about by:

1. Understanding the concept of sin. Sin is falling short of God's perfection. God created Adam and Eve perfect. They chose to disobey God's command and ate the forbidden fruit. The sin nature of mankind came from that first sin.
2. Recognizing that you are a sinner. You are a sinner by birth and by choice. If you don't believe this, then think of how you normally respond when someone hurts you, either physically or emotionally. Think of how you feel when an adult tells you that you can't do something. Think of when you want something and you steal to get it. The sin nature is in all of us.

Sinners are what we are, sin is what we do. We aren't sinners because we sin, we sin because we're sinners.
3. Believing that Jesus is the Son of God and that He died for our sins so we could be forgiven, have eternal life, and spend eternity with God. Jesus was the only perfect human because he was not born with our sin nature. He was the only sacrifice that God would accept to be offered up to wash our sins away.
4. Believing that Jesus rose (and was raised) from the dead. This is the proof that God the Father was pleased with Jesus' death for purchasing our forgiveness and restoring the ability to have a relationship with the Father. Without the resurrection, there could be no assurance of our salvation.

The believing that I speak of is not just head knowledge, as in . . . I believe that elevators are a great invention. But I never ride in one. Why would I believe that they're wonderful if I'm not willing to get in one? When I put my trust in an elevator, I get inside it, push the buttons, and expect to get to where I need to go. I've moved from believing in it to trusting in it. If I don't get in it and use it, I'll never know personally what a great invention it really is.

The same is true for Jesus. To believe He lived on earth, and maybe was a good man, and that He died a horrible death, that is just believing. To trust means that you place your trust or faith fully in Him and you do that by accepting Him as your personal Savior and Lord. You ask Him to come into your heart and life, to forgive you of your sins, and to give you eternal life. You act on your belief. Belief is the starting point, but it must find completion in faith.

> "For God so loved the world that He gave His only begotten Son, that whosoever believeth in Him should not perish, but have everlasting life."
>
> ~ John 3:16

"for all have sinned and fall short of the glory of God."

~ Roman 3:23

"For the wages of sin is death, but the free gift of God is eternal life in Christ Jesus our Lord."

~ Romans 6:23

"But God demonstrates His own love toward us, in that while we were yet sinners, Christ died for us."

~ Romans 5:8

The seven words presented in this book are an excellent tool when used in conjunction with the Bible and other tools for spiritual growth. Used alone, however, these words merely dress up and cover up the existing problem—the problem of a selfish, unregenerate heart. The words are good in order to form good habits in our lives, but habits alone won't change our hearts, lives, or eternal destination. Only the forgiveness and grace of God through our faith in the sacrificial death of Jesus can change our heart, life, and eternal destination. Won't you take that step now, if you have not already done so? At the bottom of this page is a short prayer you can use, or you can speak your own words. Whichever you choose, please say it from your heart, for that is what God looks on.

Dear Heavenly Father,

I know that I am a sinner, and that I cannot come to you because of anything I have done or can do. I can only come to you because of what Jesus did for me on the cross. He is the only way, the truth, and the life. No one comes to you except by Him. I am humbled that you love me and want to have a relationship with me, and I am thankful that you sent your Son Jesus to be the bridge between you and me. I ask you now to forgive my sins, cleanse me, and I ask you, Lord Jesus, to come into my heart and reign as King in both my heart and life. Thank you. In Jesus' name, amen.

Appendices

Appendix A—Goals and Desires

Objective: I want the bullies at school to leave me alone.
Goal: none
Desire: I want the bullies at school to leave me alone.

There is no goal because the bullies are people and their cooperation in this area is uncertain. In fact, without their cooperation and contribution in solving this problem, the problem will continue to exist.

I can take steps within the "desire," though. I can approach the bullies and tell them I do not like being tormented and ask them to stop. They most likely will laugh and continue their bullying. The best thing I can do then is to pray and ask God, not only that the bullying would stop, but also that I would have the right response to it when it happens. I could pray and ask God to help **me** understand why they choose to be mean. I could pray **for** them—that God would bless their lives and give them the things that are lacking in their lives—love, acceptance, attention, peace, joy. I can also begin to treat others as I want to be treated. If I don't like being bullied, then I won't turn around and bully someone else.

I now have a goal because the only way to effect change is by changing myself—how I see things, how I respond to others—their good or bad actions and behaviors. I can't change others, only God can change them. Only God can change **my heart** so that **I want** to develop the

personal goals of understanding others, praying for others, and respecting others.

> **Goal(s):** to be understanding of others—even those who are mean: pray for those who hurt me
> treat others with respect, kindness, and fairness
> truly live the "Golden Rule." Treat others as I want to be treated

Eventually, I may be able to tell the bullies that I care about them and that I pray for them.

The scenario on the previous page puts the power of my **responses** in **my** hands, not the bullies'. It utilizes options that are truly positive. I'm drawing boundaries and letting them know that when they bully me, they are crossing those boundaries. I'm standing up for my personhood. If they continue to disrespect my personhood and my boundaries, then I have to take the higher road. If I want a clear conscience and to know that I did everything I knew to do, I will choose to not let their hurtful words, taunts, insults, and demeaning remarks bother me. I acknowledge that I feel pain. But, I choose to let the pain go. Yes, I can let it go. I do not have to fall into their trap. When I first pray, I want to know how I should respond to them. What are positive and acceptable ways to deal with their bullying? Then, as I pray for them, my bad feelings toward them begin to lessen. I gradually begin to see them as hurt and needy people who really need love, acceptance, attention, and friendship. I begin to understand that because they are hurt, they hurt others. As I continue to pray for them, I realize I genuinely want them to experience good things and to be happy and to not hurt others. In my praying, I focus on them and what they need, rather than on my pain and my desire to be free of it.

Bullies want to be noticed and to have power. Bullies want to get you revved up. They want to get a reaction from you. The more you react to them, whether it's crying, or anger and yelling, or calling them names, or swearing at them . . . the happier they are. You just did what they wanted. Who got noticed? They did! Who has the power? They do! They are like puppeteers pulling on your strings and making you dance. If you allow them this power, the dance will be over when THEY say it's over, or when THEY get bored or tired of bullying you. When you react, and then overreact, they are very happy and you become very miserable. And who gets into trouble? YOU do! Then, they're even happier. And you carry your misery around a very long time. Unless you learn to handle your emotions and think differently about your options, you will find yourself a victim of their power and their meanness. You do have options. You need to get them thought out well in advance and determine you will use these options instead of resorting to the old familiar ways of anger, yelling, name-calling, swearing, and hitting.

Strategies for Handling Bullies or Troublemakers:
1. Ignore—
   Just let the remarks fall on "deaf ears"
2. Pray—
   Pray that you would have the courage to endure their remarks
   Pray that your nonresponse would cause them to stop
   Pray that God would bless them with what they truly need
   Pray that God might use you to influence them for good
3. Make proactive movements toward them—
   Try to be a friend to them
   Say hello to them in a pleasant manner
   Continue to ignore their hurtful remarks
   Invite them to join you in a game or to be on your team
   Write a note of encouragement to them
   Invite them to a special event, such as your birthday party

At any point you can always speak to an adult and let them know that there are students or neighborhood kids bullying you and bothering you, **especially if it is physical**—hitting, slapping, punching, kicking, knocking things out of your hands, knocking your glasses off, throwing you to the ground. Adults **should** be made aware of this level of bullying. Mean remarks and insults, however, can be dealt with in the proactive steps previously mentioned.

"Let us not listen to those who think we ought to be angry with our enemies, and who believe this to be great and manly. Nothing is so praiseworthy, nothing so clearly shows a great and noble soul, as clemency and readiness to forgive."

~ Marcus Tullius Cicero

"I shall allow no man to belittle my soul by making me hate him."

~ Booker T. Washington

"No evil propensity of the human heart is so powerful that it may not be subdued by discipline."

~ Lucius Annaeus Seneca

"When people's lives please the Lord, even their enemies are at peace with them."

~ Proverbs 16:7

"Love prospers when a fault is forgiven, but dwelling on it separates close friends."

~ Proverbs 17:9

"Don't say, 'I will get even for this wrong.' Wait for the Lord to handle the matter."

~ Proverbs 20:22

"Bless those who persecute you; bless and do not curse."

~ Romans 12:14

"Never pay back evil for evil to anyone. Respect what is right in the sight of all men."

"If possible, so far as it depends on you, be at peace with all men."

"Do not be overcome by evil, but overcome evil with good."

~ Romans 12:17–18, 21

"But I say to you, love your enemies and pray for those who persecute you."

~ Matthew 5:44

"In everything, therefore, treat people the same way you want them to treat you, for this is the Law and the Prophets."

~ Matthew 7:12

"A quarrel is quickly settled when deserted by one party; there is no battle unless there be two."

~ Lucius Annaeus Seneca

"Let them hate me, provided they respect my conduct."

~ Tiberius

"When something bad happens [to you], you have three choices. You can either let it define you, let it destroy you, or you can let it strengthen you."

~ Facebook

"Anger, if not restrained, is frequently more hurtful to us than the injury that provokes it."

~ Lucius Annaeus Seneca

"There are two ways of exerting one's strength: one is pushing down, the other is pulling up."

~ Booker T. Washington

"Wherever there is a human being, there is an opportunity for a kindness."

~ Lucius Annaeus Seneca

A Final Thought on Goals

It is possible to have *mistaken goals.* If it is your goal: 1.) to keep others busy or to get special service, 2.) to have the power, 3.) to get revenge or get even, or 4.) to give up and be left alone, then you have mistaken goals. Remember, a true goal is something you can accomplish yourself—by yourself. These mistaken goals are **desires**—something you want, but need others to help you get it. The only thing is that, by behaving in negative ways to accomplish your *mistaken goal/desire*, you are not *asking for assistance*, you are **manipulating** *the situation and others.* It is always better to simply ask for what you need, but first you have to be able to express what it is you need. Below is a list of needs that you might find helpful in determining what it is that you need.

What Do I Need From the Other Person?

Acceptance	Honor	Understanding
Answers/solutions	Order	Validation
Assistance	Patience	Worth
Assurance of love	Peace/quietness	
Chance to speak/be heard	Respect	
Encouragement	Security	
Help	To be taken seriously	
Honesty	Trust	

Appendix B—Expectations

Expectations are how I think the world, businesses, people, relationships, etc., should work. It's how I'm used to things being done. Expectations are more than preferences. They're more than comfort zones. In my thinking, expectations are how things **should** be.

Expectations can be realistic or unrealistic. Unrealistic expectations are born out of fantasy or fairy-tale beliefs—such as, Prince Charming rescues the fair maiden and they live happily ever after. Disagreements will often happen if the expectations are unrealistic. They may be unrealistic but they are on a conscious level. We are aware of them.

Most of the time, we deal with conscious expectations. But there's another level of expectations. I believe we also have subconscious expectations. These expectations can be positive or negative. Positive means you expect the good and the best; negative means you expect the bad and the worst. There is an old saying—Hope for the best but expect the worst. I just recently discovered that, subconsciously, I have always expected the worst. And I got what I expected. How interesting it is to think that if I had expected the best, how different my life might be! But I expected for my life exactly what my reality was as a child.

"If you align expectations with reality, you will never be disappointed."

~ Terrell Owens

In other words, look at your current reality. Are your parents together or apart? Is there peace and harmony in your home, or fighting, yelling, and screaming in your home? Is there respect for others or disrespect? Did either parent go to college or did they drop out of high school? Do you have relatives who are entrepreneurs, doctors, or lawyers, or do you have relatives that are gang members? Are you poor, middle class, or wealthy? If your expectations are the same as your current reality, you will have what you expect—plain and simple. And you will not be disappointed in the future. For those with the current reality of negativity, in the future, you may hate the pain and misery of your life, and you may consciously wish you had a different life. In your mind and spirit, you'll fight against being poor or being in debt, or being fired, or being in jail, or losing your friends or family. You may lash out in anger at others, and the "system," and God for wronging you or disappointing you, but unless your subconscious expectations are changed, you will reap what has been sown.

So many people expect to have a bad, hard, painful, suffering existence. If this is your thinking and your expectations, you **can** turn it around. Just begin sowing a different "crop." Challenge the expectations, and then change them. Begin saying "I expect the best," or "I expect good things in my life." And pray, believing that God truly loves you and that He cares for and provides for His children. Expect and believe that God only brings or allows into your life what is ultimately for your good and His glory. Sometimes He may bring or allow bad things into your life, but you can still believe that it can be for your good and His glory. God does not destroy His creation. Satan does that. But God can work through the most painful times of your life, especially your childhood, teaching you wonderful lessons and making something beautiful out of your life. Put God on the throne of your life and you will have joy, peace, and contentment.

"Your expectations open or close the doors of your supply. If you expect grand things and work honestly for them, they will come to you. Your supply will correspond with your expectation."

~ Orison Swett Marden

"Being in control of your life and having realistic expectations about your day—to—day challenges are the keys to stress management, which is perhaps the most important ingredient to living a happy, healthy, and rewarding life."

~ Marilu Henner

"We tend to live up to our expectations."

~ Earl Nightingale

"Never idealize others. They will never live up to your expectations."

~ Leo Buscaglia

"If you accept the expectations of others, especially negative ones, then you will never change the outcome."

~ Michael Jordan

"Many people feel so pressured by the expectations of others that it causes them to be frustrated, miserable, and confused about what they should do. But there is a way to live a simple, joy-filled, peaceful life, and the key is learning how to be led by the Holy Spirit, not the traditions or expectations of man."

~ Joyce Meyer

"Don't lower your expectations to meet your performance. Raise your level of performance to meet your expectations. Expect the best of yourself, and then do what is necessary to make it a reality."

~ Ralph Marston

"Our environment, the world in which we live and work, is a mirror of our attitudes and expectations."

~ Earl Nightingale

"I am not in this world to live up to other people's expectations, nor do I feel that the world must live up to mine."

~ Fritz Perls

"Lower your expectations of earth. This isn't heaven, so don't expect it to be."

~ Max Lucado

Appendix C—Disappointment

Disappointment is inevitable. It's how we handle it that is the more important issue. If we're victims, then we see it as confirming our victim status. If we attempt to chase mistaken goals, then those goals will be blocked and we will become angry, frustrated, and disappointed. If our expectations are of the bad and the worst, then disappointment confirms our negative expectations. If our expectations idealize certain people, then they will fail us and disappointment will hit us hard. Even if our lives are good and happy, disappointment will come sometime.

How do we deal with disappointment? How do we lessen the pain and the extreme sadness that it can cause? I think we have to recognize each disappointment as a loss of something. Seeing it as a loss, we can then grieve it. We must feel the pain and sadness and take the time to grieve.

In a previous chapter I mention a time when my father disappointed me. I was around nine or ten. In the years that followed, I expected my father to be just who he was . . . nothing more, nothing different. I expected more rejection from him, and I got it. When I turned eighteen, he sent a letter to the court stating that he was no longer financially responsible for me. No birthday card, no present, no happy birthday phone call, just this formal, impersonal letter. I never grieved. I never knew I needed to, because I didn't know I was emotionally wounded. What I expected of him all those years kept me from being hurt and disappointed on my eighteenth birthday. I expected him to behave at his worst. I knew he was not a good provider, and I expected him to walk away from further responsibility. When I expected the worst and I got it, I was not hurt or disappointed. Or so I thought.

When I recently became aware of my subconscious expectations, and that I expected the worst, it became clear why I didn't grieve. When I realized that I had shielded myself from further disappointment by expecting the worst from him, and that my father's rejection really did affect me, I was able, now, to feel the hurt and sadness. And, believe me, I felt it. I cried for quite a while. I grieved that I was rejected and abandoned. I grieved that I didn't have the father that I wanted or needed.

Something else came out of this. In my expecting the worst, I expected God to treat me the same way. Too many times it seemed like I got what I expected. But, seeing God as behaving the same as flawed people is not seeing the true God. One cannot know the real God if one's perception is skewed. This is why we need to confront our misperceptions and misconceptions and begin to think rightly about God. We can think rightly about God only by reading the Bible.

"If we will be quiet and ready enough, we shall find compensation in every disappointment."

~ Henry David Thoreau

"The principles of living greatly include the capacity to face trouble with courage, disappointment with cheerfulness, and trial with humility."

~ Thomas S. Monson

"We must accept finite disappointment, but never lose infinite hope."

~ Martin Luther King, Jr.

"Disappointment is inevitable. But to become discouraged, there's a choice I make. God would never discourage me. He would always point me to himself to trust him. Therefore, my discouragement is from Satan. As you go through the emotions that we have, hostility is not from God, bitterness, unforgiveness, all of these are attacks from Satan."

~ Charles Stanley

"Disenchantment, whether it is a minor disappointment or a major shock, is the signal that things are moving into transition in our lives."

~ William Throsby Bridges

"Burning desire to be or do something gives us staying power—a reason to get up every morning or to pick ourselves up and start in again after a disappointment."

~ Marsha Sinetar

"Enthusiasm is followed by disappointment and even depression, and then by renewed enthusiasm."

~ Murray Gell-Mann

"Depression begins with disappointment. When disappointment festers in the soul, it leads to discouragement."

~ Joyce Meyer

"Sometimes when you get disappointment it makes you stronger."

~ David Rudisha

"The more we shelter children from every disappointment, the more devastating future disappointments will be."

~ Fred G. Gosman

"When we focus on our gratitude, the tide of disappointment goes out and the tide of love rushes in."

~ Kristin Armstrong

Appendix D—Taking Up Defenses

Taking up defenses means that you are tattling about something said or done toward another person. You're trying to defend someone because the offense bothered you. However, if the person it was directed to didn't see or hear it, or he chose to let it go, then you have no need to defend the person. If it doesn't matter to someone else, why should it matter to you? Defending those who have no voice or can't speak for themselves is admirable and noble. We must stand up and be their voice. But those who have a voice must learn to speak on their own behalf, and must learn when it is appropriate to do so. We all must learn to recognize who has a voice and who does not.

It is also possible to **perceive** that a wrong was done by an adult (teacher) toward a student, and to take up a defense for that student. This is a faulty perception, because the adult is most likely working with that student to improve their understanding of course work and to be able to pass tests. There is no reason to complain and argue that the other student is being treated unfairly or being forced or coerced into working. There is no reason to become angry and to defend students that are willing to put in the hard work. Again, if it is not bothering the students in question, then lay down your sword. You have nothing to defend.

Appendix E—Taking Up Offenses

Taking up offenses is when your opinion and treatment of someone is changed negatively because they offended or wronged someone you know —a friend or a family member. You may see or hear it personally, or your friend or family member may tell you. Then, you get upset and carry the offense as if it happened directly to you. You take it personally. You might feel that you were hurt. You then become angry. Even if your friend/family member and the other person get it straightened out, you still want to hold onto it. Again, why hold on to something that is none of your concern? Carrying around defenses and offenses that rightfully belong to others, and have nothing to do with you, leads to pent-up anger at those you feel are guilty, an intense sense of injustice and the belief that your judgment and justice should be measured out on the guilty parties, and bitterness as well. Believe me, you do not want to grow into adulthood with lots of anger, severe judgment, and bitterness firmly rooted in your life.

I believe the root of taking up defenses and offenses is the desire to be in control. We feel we know best, we know what is right and wrong for everyone, and what we want to happen should happen. Perhaps there is the feeling that the harmed one needs more assistance or more advice, or just another person to be on their side. But we are not in control of these situations and circumstances. We are only in control of ourselves . . . our emotions, our thoughts, and our choices. Rather than being angry and vengeful on behalf of someone else, we could pray for the others involved, and we could trust that the adults who are in charge really know what they're doing.

Appendix F—Strategies for HALT

Hurt, **A**ngry, **L**onely, **T**ired

Below is a list of strategies to employ when feeling hurt, angry, tired, and/or lonely. Choose to change your thinking and your emotions will follow.

- Walk away from the problem/situation/person
- Go to a quiet place
- Relax your body—unclench your fists and your jaws
- Take slow, deep breaths—in and out
- Count to ten
- Think about what's good, noble, pure, and positive
- Do some exercises—push-ups, jumping jacks, toe touches, etc.
- Talk to an adult with the intention of working through your feelings, rather than the intention of the adult solving the problem or punishing the other person
- Make a plan with another person to help each other when you are experiencing these feelings
- Talk to God—express your hurt, anger, loneliness, or tiredness to Him
- Ask God or yourself why this hurts you, angers you, or bothers you and listen for the answer

- Let go of the intensity of your emotions
- Learn to laugh—not at others or their mistakes—but use laughter as a way to get out of your anger and frustration; watch a funny movie or read a joke book

"A joyful heart is good medicine, but a broken spirit dries up the bones."

~ Proverbs 17:22

Appendix G—Thinking/Reacting

Below are two lists that illustrate this idea of thinking vs. reacting.

THINKING SIDE	REACTING SIDE
Think first before you act	Impulsive – just act
Pause – stay calm	No pause – keep on going
In control	Not in control
Positive/right choices	Negative/wrong choices
Responsible	Irresponsible
Consider rights of others	Consider only my rights
Consider consequences	Consider immediate gratification
See the big picture	See only my little world
Understand the hurts of others	Understand only my hurt
Desire empathy, understanding, mercy, and forgiveness for all involved	Desire to be vindicated, appeased, justified, applauded, and winner

Anonymous

Appendix H—Requiring More of Yourself

More Quotes for Better Thoughts

"The best way to dispel negative thoughts is to require that they have a purpose."

~ Robert Brault

"If you don't like something change it; if you can't change it, change the way you think about it."

~ Mary Engelbreit

"Think big thoughts but relish small pleasures."

~ H. Jackson Brown, Jr., *Life's Little Instruction Book*

"Every thought is a seed. If you plant crab apples, don't count on harvesting Golden Delicious."

~ Bill Meyer

"To be wronged is nothing unless you continue to remember it."

~ Confucius

"Reject your sense of injury and the injury itself disappears."

~ Marcus Aurelius

"I think, what has this day brought me, and what have I given it?"

~ Henry Moore

"Whenever anyone has offended me, I try to raise my soul so high that the offense cannot reach it."

~ Rene Descartes

"No life is so hard that you can't make it easier by the way you take it."

~ Ellen Glasgow

"If you keep on saying things are going to be bad, you have a good chance of becoming a prophet."

~ Isaac Bashevis Singer

"Think before you speak. Read before you think."

~ Fran Lebowitz

"He who thinks little errs much . . ."

~ Leonardo da Vinci

"There is nothing as remarkable as learning how to think better."

~ Anonymous

"Let not your mind run on what you lack as much as what you already have."

~ Marcus Aurelius

More Quotes for Better Attitudes

"A happy person is not a person in a certain set of circumstances, but rather a person with a certain set of attitudes."

~ Hugh Downs

"Attitudes are contagious. Are yours worth catching?"

~ Dennis and Wendy Mannering

"It's so hard when I have to, and so easy when I want to."

~ Ann Gottlier

"There is nothing so easy but that it becomes difficult when you do it reluctantly."

~ Publius Terentius Afer

"Defeat is not bitter unless you swallow it."

~ Joe Clark

"The only disability in life is a bad attitude."

~ Scott Hamilton

"No power in society, no hardship in your condition can depress you, keep you down, in knowledge, power, virtue, influence, but by your own consent."

~ William Ellery Channing, 1838

"When you feel dog tired at night, it may be because you've growled all day long."

~ Anonymous

"We awaken in others the same attitude of mind we hold toward them."

~ Elbert Hubbard

"Weakness of attitude becomes weakness of character."

~ Albert Einstein

"You have power over your mind—not outside events. Realize this and you will find strength."

~ Marcus Aurelius

"I certainly don't regret my experiences because without them, I couldn't imagine who or where I'd be today. Life is an amazing gift to those who have overcome great obstacles, and attitude is everything!"

~ Sasha Azevedo

"Ninety-nine percent of the failures come from people who have the habit of making excuses."

~ George Washington Carver

"How we think shows through in how we act. Attitudes are mirrors of the mind. They reflect thinking."

~ David Joseph Schwartz

More Quotes for Better Beliefs

"You can't change the fruit without changing the root."

~ Stephen R. Covey

A tree is known by its fruit. "So every good tree bears good fruit, but the bad tree bears bad fruit."

~ Matthew 7:17

"Do not be deceived, God is not mocked; for whatever a man sows, this he will also reap."

~ Galatians 6:7

"The chief end of man is to glorify God and to enjoy him forever."

~ Westminster Shorter Catechism

"For my part I believe in the forgiveness of sin and the redemption of ignorance."

~ Adlai Stevenson

"Very often a change of self is needed more than a change of scene."

~ Arthur Christopher Benson

"The way we see the problem is the problem."

~ Stephen R. Covey

"It is always better to have no ideas than false ones; to believe nothing than to believe what is wrong."

~ Thomas Jefferson

More Quotes for Better Speech

"It is by the goodness of God that in our country we have those three unspeakably precious things: freedom of speech, freedom of conscience, and the prudence never to practice either of them."

~ Mark Twain

"When words are many, sin is not absent, but he who holds his tongue is wise."

~ Proverbs 10:19

"From the fruit of his lips a man is filled with good things as surely as the work of his hands rewards him."

~ Proverbs 12:14

"A man of knowledge uses words with restraint, and a man of understanding is even-tempered."
"Even a fool is thought wise if he keeps silent, and discerning if he holds his tongue."

~ Proverbs 17:27–28

"It is to a man's honor to avoid strife, but every fool is quick to quarrel."

~ Proverbs 20:3

"He who guards his mouth and his tongue keeps himself from calamity."

~ Proverbs 21:23

"A fortune made by a lying tongue is a fleeting vapor and a deadly snare."

~ Proverbs 21:6

"He who restrains his words has knowledge, and he who has a cool spirit is a man of understanding."

~ Proverbs 17:27

More Quotes for Better Actions

"You are the embodiment of the information you choose to accept and act upon. To change your circumstances you need to change your thinking and subsequent actions."

~ Adlin Sinclair

"If you continue to do what you've always done, you'll continue to have what you've always had."

~ Anonymous

"Do you want to know who you are? Don't ask. Act! Action will delineate and define you."

~ Thomas Jefferson

"He who walks with wise men will be wise, but the companion of fools will suffer harm."

~ Proverbs 13:20

"He who is slow to anger has great understanding, but he who is quick-tempered exalts folly."

~ Proverbs 14:29

More Quotes for Better Work

"I have been impressed with the urgency of doing. Knowing is not enough; we must apply. Being willing is not enough; we must do."

~ Leonardo da Vinci

"Nothing ever comes to one that is worth having, except as a result of hard work."

~ Booker T. Washington

"Gardens are not made by sitting in the shade."

~ English Proverb

"Time lost is time lost. It's gone forever. Some people tell themselves that they will work twice as hard tomorrow to make up for what they did not do today. People should always do their best. If they work twice as hard tomorrow, then they should have also worked twice as hard today. That would have been their best."

- John Wooden

"Never put off till tomorrow what you can do today."

- Thomas Jefferson

"Study while others are sleeping; work while others are loafing; prepare while others are playing; and dream while others are wishing."

- William Arthur Ward

"What we do on some great occasion will probably depend on what we already are: and what we are will be the result of previous years of self-discipline."

- H. P. Liddon

"It is not by muscle, speed, or physical dexterity that great things are achieved, but by reflection, force of character, and judgment."

- Marcus Tullius Cicero

"Work hard because you never know who is watching."

- Anonymous

Appendix I—Winning and Losing

There is a mind-set these days that everyone should be a winner and that no one should lose. In one sense this can be true. For instance, in a marathon even the last person to cross the finish line is a winner because that person endured through the whole marathon and did not quit until he/she crossed the finish line. This is to win on a personal level because this person was competing more against himself. That person may want to win, but knows that realistically, he has little chance of being the first to cross the finish line. He's just happy and proud that he made it that far.

However, the fault in the belief that everyone is a winner no matter what is that when you compete against others or are on a team competing against another team, there will be a decisive winner and a definite loser. There is an important element to consider, and that is good sportsmanship. Of course, it's always great to win, but winning alone will not teach you how to be modest and grateful. Winning is liable to teach you to be proud, arrogant, conceited, and manipulative.

When you experience losing, you are put in a position to make a choice. When you choose to be a gracious loser, you are learning good sportsmanship and developing the determination to improve and to do better the next time.

No one wants to lose all the time, but we all have to realize that sometimes we will lose. It's not the end of the world if we lose. We can learn to accept that this time we were defeated, and we can lose gracefully, and then move on. There's no need to brood about it, or to begin thinking negatively about ourselves, or to pick fights with others, or to let it consume us. It is simply one more thing that should be let go.

Appendix J—Respect

What is respect? Is it the same for everyone? What does it look like? How do I know if I'm being respectful or not? How do I know if I am being respected or disrespected by someone?

Dictionary.com says this of respect:

Respect: noun;
#3 esteem for or a sense of the worth or excellence of a person, a personal quality or ability or something considered as a manifestation of a personal quality or ability. I have great respect for her judgment.

#4 deference to a right, privilege, privileged position, or someone or something considered to have certain rights or privileges; proper acceptance and courtesy; acknowledgment: respect for a suspect's right to counsel; to show respect for the flag; respect for the elderly.

verb (used with object);
#9 to hold in esteem or honor: I cannot respect a cheat.
#10 to show regard or consideration for: to respect someone's rights.
#11 to refrain from intruding upon or interfering with: to respect a person's privacy.

There are many parts involved in showing respect. My belief concerning respect is: People are created in the image of God, therefore,

- Respect their right to live,
- Respect their purpose or direction in life,
- Respect their ideas, opinions, values, and beliefs,
- Respect their emotions and feelings,
- Respect their choices,
- Respect their personal space,
- Respect their privacy,
- Respect their possessions and property.

I think that each person sees respect in a different way. What I consider respectful or disrespectful to me may be nothing like what someone else considers respectful or disrespectful. I believe that the way each person views respect and disrespect is related to what each person's emotional needs are. One of my emotional needs is to be heard. Being a parent, this means hear what I say, and if I gave instructions, then please follow through. I don't like repeating myself over and over, and I feel disrespected when my words have not been heard and acted on.

There are, however, general rules of respect. You should respect:

- Your elders (anyone older than you)
- Those in **positions of authority** over you (any adult in charge of you and your well-being)
- Your peers
- Possessions and property
- Nature

Those in positions of authority you may not like personally, but you should always respect them for the position they hold.

Respecting nature means that when you're outside walking or playing, you respect the animals' right to exist because you're in their habitat. Don't try to kill them or step on them because you can or because you want to feel powerful or because you just don't like them. God created all creatures, and we are to be good stewards and respectful of all life.

CPSIA information can be obtained
at www.ICGtesting.com
Printed in the USA
FFOW02n1241190315
11994FF